Hideo Yamaki

Translated by
Clyde Newton

Discover Sumo

*Stories from
Yobidashi Hideo*

GENDAI SHOKAN

Discover Sumo
Stories from Yobidashi Hideo

2017年1月8日　第1版第1刷発行

山木秀男 著

©2016, Hideo Yamaki
©2017, GENDAI SHOKAN PUBLISHING CO., LTD.

Publishing office:
GENDAI SHOKAN PUBLISHING CO., LTD.
3-2-5 Iidabashi Chiyoda-ku, Tokyo 102-0072 Japan
Tel: +81-(0)3-3221-1321　Fax: +81-(0)3-3262-5906

Printed by:
Hirakawa Kogyosha Co., Ltd.
Tokoinsatsujo

Binder:
Sekishindo Co., Ltd.

Translator:
Clyde Newton

Proofreader:
Teiko Sato

Illustrator:
Ayamorikemuri

Book design:
Shigeaki Ito

Printed in Japan　ISBN978-4-7684-5798-6
定価はカバーに表示してあります。
乱丁・落丁本はおとりかえいたします。
禁無断転載
The price is indicated on the cover.
Any copies with damage or missing pages will be replaced.
All rights reserved

Foreword
Life as a Yobidashi from My Entrance into Isegahama Beya to Retirement

Hideo

December 27, 2014 marked the end of my 45 years as a yobidashi.

I had no special interest in becoming a yobidashi*. My grades were falling in my second year of high school. Further, I was tired of hearing about the campus strife of that era, and thus I did not give much thought to going on to university. I thought about what I should do in the future. As I was interested in local scenery and customs and did not give much thought to money, I thought it would be good if I could find work which would enable me to travel all around Japan. Just as

I was thinking the theater might be a good choice, among various possibilities, I remembered that my father often went to see sumo and that he knew someone in the koenkai* (supporter's association) of Isegahama Beya*. Sumo had jungyo* (regional tours) that traveled throughout Japan. That having been said, it would impossible to become a rikishi* without having an impressive physique. I had seen gyoji* on television, but thought their movements were too stiff and formal. Simply stated, that is what led me to think becoming a yobidashi might be the answer.

However, I had not voiced any of these thoughts to my parents in the third and final year of high school. I did submit a request for university application forms, though. I ended up becoming a ronin (having a gap year) for one year. I was born in Shimoda-shi in Shizuoka-ken, and at that time with many buses touring the Izu Peninsula, I realized that my region had no industries other than tourism, thus I should become a yobidashi after all. I placed a letter saying I wanted to become a yobidashi in the briefcase which my father, a schoolteacher, took with him to work every day. Two or three days later, my father asked me whether I really wanted to become a yobidashi. I thought he might be con-

Foreword: Life as a Yobidashi from My Entrance into Isegahama Beya to Retirement

cerned as I was seeking an unusual occupation, but he expressed no opposition. I was the youngest child, with two elder brothers and one elder sister, so perhaps that factored in my father's response.

In February 1969, my father took me to Isegahama Beya in Tokyo's Ryogoku area, and there we met Isegahama Oyakata*, former Yokozuna* Terukuni. In the prewar era, he broke the record for being the youngest yokozuna, achieving promotion at the age of 23 years and four months. This record was not surpassed until after the September 1961 tournament, when Taiho (21 years and three months old) and Kashiwado (22 years and nine months old) were jointly promoted to yokozuna.

Although the oyakata was a large man, his choice of words was polite and gentle. This did not change even after I entered the heya*.

The oyakata asked me to try calling in the manner of a yobidashi, and I did so. He then said, "That's quite good, isn't it? I will tell the senior yobidashi." That's how things were decided and I began my career as a yobidashi of Isegahama Beya. The heya also housed Kiyokuni and former Sekiwake* Kairyuyama, who was then serving as an oyakata attached to the heya and as a shobu shimpan* (judge). Kiyokuni made an impressive effort in the May 1969 tournament, and was promoted to ozeki* for the July tournament. It was a time when Isegahama Beya was doing very well.

The senior yobidashi the oyakata was referring to was Kotaro-san* of Isegahama Beya. As my real name is Yamaki Hidehito, Kotaro-san gave me the name of Yobidashi Hideo. As the second kanji character in my real name is difficult to read, he changed the kanji to a more easily read one, which means man. This was all very easy to understand and there is no deep meaning in the name.

The top yobidashi of the time was Kankichi-san. Immediately below him were Kenichi-san, Minezo-san, Zenzaburo-san, and Norio-san.

I made my debut in the March tournament of 1969. I remember receiving instructions, such as "This is the shikiri* line, so you need to stand here before you reach it," from my seniors Teruo-san and Saburo-san at a jungyo held in Tatsuno-shi in Hyogo-ken.

I made my debut on the dohyo* in a hombasho* (official tournament) in May 1969. I was told that I would be appearing on the dohyo that day, and my response was just

Foreword: Life as a Yobidashi from My Entrance into Isegahama Beya to Retirement

"Yes." Before I set foot on the dohyo, I did not even know in which direction I should gaze when I was up there. I had no time to spare and did not even know who was close to me. It was a strange feeling, but I knew I could not make a mistake. However, somehow, I was able to get through it without incident. The number of bouts I had to attend to continued even beyond the fifth and sixth ones. At the time, the maximum number of yobidashi was set at 38, but including me, there were only 23, and thus I had to handle a large number of bouts. Nowadays, the number of rikishi has fallen while the yobidashi have increased. There were only about half as many yobidashi when I started as there are now. By the way, the number of yobidashi is now set at 45.

One of the memories of my youth is the sumo coach on the railways. It was a reserved train for the sumo group, and was used for tournaments outside Tokyo and for jungyo. Although there was a first-class coach available, the lower-ranked participants used cars with open floors. For longer journeys during jungyo, we bought newspapers, and spread them out over the floor for us to sit on. When we spent the night in trains, it was easier to sleep on the newspapers rather than directly on the floor. Those days are gone now. The

Shinkansen (bullet trains) or buses are used for travel, and have proper seats for everybody.

Further, I did something foolish which resulted in me being injured. It was the Osaka Basho* in March. It was 8:00 p.m., a time when there are no tasks a yobidashi needs to handle. So I decided to go out by myself and have some fun. Yobidashi have a considerable amount of freedom, unlike rikishi. A young rikishi, of about my age, who envied me, hid my bag to prevent me from going out. So we decided to settle matters with a sumo bout. The kid was young, but all the same a rikishi. I was just a small yobidashi, so taking him on was recklessness on my part. With much effort, I was able to lift the young rikishi up. Unfortunately one of the panels in the floor of our lodgings was missing, and the moment I lifted him up, my foot got caught there. With the weight of both of us falling on me, I ended up with a multiple fracture of my left ankle. I was able to leave hospital during the May tournament, but I was absent from the entire basho. The rikishi I fought with that day never made sekitori* status. I have never since done sumo with a rikishi.

Even though I went through this kind of incident, I gained experience over the years, and when yobidashi were listed on the banzuke* from the July tournament of 1994, I was given jumaime yobidashi status. From there, I rose to makuuchi yobidashi, sanyaku yobidashi, fukutate yobidashi, and in the January tournament of 2008 I was given the ultimate promotion to tate yobidashi. During these years, Isegahama Beya closed, and I was transferred to Kiriyama Beya. However, in 2011, Kiriyama Beya also closed and I moved to Asahiyama Beya, and it was there that I reached retirement age.

My last task as a yobidashi was the bout in which Hakuho-zeki* clinched the championship on the final day of the Kyushu Basho in November 2014. It was a bout I will never forget. My high school classmates had come to Fukuoka to see me, and an NHK TV broadcast depicted my final days as a yobidashi. After my last bout, Hakuho-zeki gave me a bouquet of flowers and three of the kensho* prizes he had won. I think he said something like "Thank you for all your efforts," and I just replied "Thank you," not being able to say anything else. I regret that. I wanted to say more to Hakuho-zeki, but he had to prepare for the awards ceremony immediately. However, our eyes met firmly, and I think I was able to express the feelings I had in my heart.

Reflecting back on my life as a yobidashi, I am glad, above all else, that I was able to serve without incident until reaching retirement age. Sumo, however, continues forever. To think that I am no longer involved makes me a bit sad.

Based on my experiences, I would like to explain the fundamentals of sumo to everyone who is interested.

*Words highlighted by asterisks are defined in the list of sumo terms from p. 171.

Table of contents

1 Foreword
Life as a Yobidashi from
My Entrance into Isegahama Beya to Retirement

Chapter 1

13 Let's Start with Discussion of the Urakata

14 The People Who Support Sumo

16 The Yobidashi are in Charge of Calling the Rikishi as Well as Sweeping Dohyo

19 I Only Thought I Called Out Well on Three Days in An Entire Tournament

26 The Cheat Sheet Used by Yobidashi

27 Taiko
——Yaguradaiko and Furedaiko are Important Tasks for the Yobidashi

32 Constructing the Dohyo——Manual Labor by All the Yobidashi

42 We Have Many Tasks to Fulfill, Including Hitting Wooden Clappers and Carrying Kensho Banners

47 The Daily Life of a Yobidashi——in My Case

50 The Taikozuka
——Performing Religious Services for the Souls of Departed Yobidashi

51 Gyoji——Sumo's Referees-Judging Bouts is Their First Responsibility

55 Gunbai——Essential Item for Gyoji

59 Gyoji Handle the Public Address System

62 Presenting the Kaobure——Done by the Gyoji and Yobidashi

64 The Banzuke is Written in Sumoji

67 Gyoji Wear Different Costumes According to Their Rank

70 The Tokoyama's Work
——They Become Full-Fledged When They Can Arrange Oichomage

73 Former Rikishi Become Wakaimonogashira and Sewanin

Chapter 2
Sumo's Leading Actors- Rikishi and Oyakata

- 76 What is Needed to Become a Rikishi
- 82 The Promotion of Rikishi
  ——Those Who Reach Jumaime are Called Sekitori
- 90 Shikona——A Rikishi's Ring Name, Real Names are Acceptable
- 92 Mawashi——A Rikishi Loses if his Mawashi Comes Off
- 98 A Day in the Life of a Rikishi——Keiko Is Done Only in the Morning
- 101 Chanko——If There is Not Enough Chankosen
- 104 Dohyoiri——The Sekitori Show Their Faces
- 109 Bouts——From Entering Shitakubeya to Leaving
- 116 Torikumi are Decided Upon Every Day
- 117 There are Currently 82 Winning Techniques
- 119 The Yumitorishiki——A Ceremony Performed on Behalf of the Winner
- 122 Yusho, the Sansho and Kenshokin
  ——The Makuuchi Yusho Winner Receives Prize Money of 10 Million Yen
- 127 Jungyo and Hanazumo

132 Rikishi I Remember —— Hokutenyu Had Style

134 To Become an Oyakata, One Must Succeed to One of the 105 Toshiyori Myoseki

136 Oyakata Operating Heya and Oyakata Belonging to Heya

139 Okamisan Have a Role Akin to that of Mothers

141 Managers

141 Koenkai —— Membership is Available from 10,000 Yen Upwards

143 There are Six Ichimon

Chapter 3

145 Enjoying Sumo

146 Sumo is Said to Have Originated with Nomi no Sukune

153 From the Edo Era to Today
 —— There was a Crisis After the Meiji Restoration

158 Nihon Sumo Kyokai

162 Seeing Sumo Beya —— Watching Keiko

164 Watching Sumo at the Kokugikan

169 In Conclusion

171 Glossary

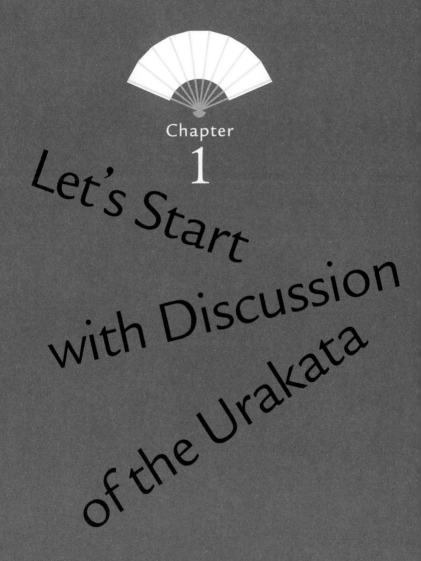

Chapter 1

Let's Start with Discussion of the Urakata

The People Who Support Sumo

It goes without saying that the leading role in sumo is taken by the rikishi who clash on the dohyo to seek the championship. It can also be said that the oyakata, or elders, play a key role in training those rikishi and sending them to the dohyo. However, these men alone do not comprise the entire world of sumo. As in any other profession, sumo also needs the support of urakata, or behind-the-scenes people. Gyoji hold a gunbai* (war fan) in their hands and call out "hakkyoi, nokotta, nokotta" as they judge bouts between rikishi. Yobidashi hold a fan while they call rikishi onto the dohyo, saying, "higashiii...xxumiii," while tokoyama* arrange the mage* (topknots) of rikishi. Wakaimonogashira* (or wakaimongashira) manage rikishi in the makushita* and below (who at this level are officially classified as just being trainees), while sewanin* handle and store equipment needed for sumo matches. All of these people work hard to support the sumo world.

Wakaimonogashira and sewanin positions are all taken by former rikishi. In the past, some gyoji, yobidashi, and tokoyama were former rikishi, but this is no longer allowed.

When I entered sumo, it was said that those seeking

Chapter 1: Let's Start with Discussion of the Urakata

prestige should become gyoji, those wanting money should become yobidashi, and those seeking fun should become tokoyama. This makes it look like yobidashi earn a lot of money, and in the distant past, such was actually the case. For example, yobidashi used to sell souvenirs at sumo tournaments, and those earnings added up. Such additional income resulted in the above expression about yobidashi making money, but by the time I entered sumo, we were no longer selling souvenirs and other things at tournaments. We now have a salary system. I think gyoji earn more salary than the other behind-the-scenes people. Gyoji who entered sumo around the same time as I did earned a little more than I did in their first year. Further, the high prestige of being a gyoji remains unchanged from the past.

As far as "tokoyama having fun" is concerned, it is not that they do not work hard. I will explain this in more detail later, but in addition to calling rikishi to the dohyo, yobidashi have many other tasks to perform. Gyoji do not only judge bouts. On the other hand, the only work that tokoyama do is arranging the hair of rikishi. Since they only have work to do when rikishi need their hair arranged, the above expression about them having fun came into being.

The Yobidashi are in Charge of Calling the Rikishi as Well as Sweeping the Dohyo

My job was to be a yobidashi, one of the behind-the-scenes men. As you can see at the Kokugikan or when you watch sumo on television, yobidashi can be seen calling out rikishi, sweeping the dohyo, carrying the prize banners around the dohyo, and handing the gyoji prize money. All of the yobidashi wear kimono and tattsukebakama* (men's formal divided skirts with the cuffs tied by cord) with the names of corporate sponsors written on them. Some people may think that yobidashi just call rikishi, but such is not the case.

Three key tasks are handled by the yobidashi; calling out rikishi, maintaining and constructing the dohyo, or dohyotsuki, and taiko* (drumming). Other work includes

Chapter 1: Let's Start with Discussion of the Urakata

Three key tasks

1. Calling out rikishi
2. Constructing the dohyo
3. Drumming

Hitting wooden clappers

Sprinkling water

There are also many other tasks for yobidashi.

Carrying the prize banners around the dohyo

Sweeping the dohyo

17

hitting wooden clappers (ki or hyoshigi) together, carrying the prize banners around the dohyo, sprinkling water when the dohyo becomes dry, and sweeping sand on the dohyo. We work hard during the tournaments.

When I entered the sumo world, there were few rules pertaining to becoming a yobidashi, and with just one phone call, I was simply told to come every day after a certain date. Today, there is a training period of one tournament, set at the discretion of a senior yobidashi who acts as a supervisor. Some recruits turn out to suitable, while others do not, though actually almost all are found to be ok. This also applies to both gyoji and tokoyama.

Yobidashi have a ranking system. The present system, as revised in November 1994, consists of, in order of ranking from the bottom upwards, jonokuchi yobidashi, jonidan yobidashi, sandanme yobidashi, makushita yobidashi, jumaime yobidashi, makuuchi yobidashi, sanyaku yobidashi, fukutate yobidashi, and tate yobidashi. There are limits on the number of yobidashi at the jumaime* level and above, which are, respectively, up to eight, up to seven, three, one, and one, and the total number of yobidashi at all levels is set at 45.

Chapter 1: Let's Start with Discussion of the Urakata

I mentioned jumaime yobidashi above. Rikishi and gyoji are formally termed as being jumaime, however, on television and other media, this is referred to simply as juryo*. I think the word juryo is more familiar to everyone. In the old days, it is said that rikishi in the top 10 ranks of the makushita were paid 10 ryo (currency used in Japan in the Edo Era [1603-1868]), however, it is not known whether this was actually true. Rikishi in the jumaime and above are referred to as sekitori. Hereafter in this book, I will use the formal term of jumaime.

I Only Thought I Called Out Well on Three Days in An Entire Tournament

The most readily visible role of the yobidashi is calling out rikishi's names. In the old days, there was a division of labor among the tasks handled by yobidashi. There were even yobidashi who never called out, but from January 1965, all yobidashi began to call out names.

It can be said that a bout between rikishi begins with yobidashi calling out names. Yobidashi mount the dohyo, call out the names of the rikishi who will next vie with each other from the higashi (east) and nishi (west) sides, after which the rikishi themselves step up on the dohyo. On odd numbered days after the first day, yobidashi unfold their white fans and turn to higashi to call rikishi from that side first, and on even numbered days, they turn to nishi. The call begins with "higashiii... xxumiii, xxumiii."

High ranking people in the Nihon Sumo Kyokai (Japan Sumo Association) told me they had received letters asking why yobidashi use a fan when they call out names. I replied that I did not know why. Troubled about this, I added that "Without a fan, it would probably not look proper." Somebody then opinioned that fans were used to prevent the yobidashi's spittle from flying towards the waiting rikishi. Actually, I do not really know why fans are used.

Normally, yobidashi call the names of rikishi in bouts of the sanyaku* level and above twice. Gyoji Kimura Shonosuke XXVIII (whose real name was Goto Satoru) held that this applied only to honwari bouts (official tournament bouts as announced the previous day by the bout compilation committee of the judging department), and did not include playoff bouts. This policy of not calling the names of rikishi in playoff bouts twice has been followed since then. As we normally call the names of rikishi at this level twice,

Chapter 1: Let's Start with Discussion of the Urakata

our pace was somewhat disrupted. At first, Yobidashi Kankichi-san had considerable difficulty with this.

The tate yobidashi calls only the final bout. Other yobidashi call two bouts. However, if I had wanted to, I could have done 20 bouts a day.

Actually, nobody is really tasked with providing guidance in calling out names. We learn and improve our skills by watching and imitating. As I realized when it came my turn to provide instruction, voice is not something that depends upon logic, and thus cannot be taught. We can ask others to watch and imitate us, but there is no guarantee that they will be able to match us perfectly, and this may change according to the way they comprehend what they are taught.

We were told to call from our abdomens. I didn't know how, but I got a knack for doing this by singing enka (Japanese traditional songs). It was my own style of abdominal breathing. Calling from one's abdomen does not hurt the throat. This is just my personal theory, but I think calling out names is enka. I don't think I would do well in singing new music. The inflection in calling names matches that of enka. I can sing any enka songs, starting with those of Kitajima Saburo-san, and as for female singers, I like Shimazu

Aya-san. Her songs are easy to sing.

We were not taught timing by word of mouth. The gap between higashi or nishi and the name of the rikishi is important, and this timing is especially important when we call out names twice. We can't have either too long or too short a gap between the words. This can only be mastered through experience. If one handles the gaps poorly, they tend to become too wide. This is the same kind of thing as one's lines in a dramatic performance. Without singing enka, I think one tends to handle these gaps poorly. My impression was that Eitaro-san's calling was charming.

During the Tochi-Waka Era (the days of Yokozuna Tochinishiki and Wakanohana I), I saw Kotetsu-san on television. When he called out, the audience became quiet. If the crowd was noisy, his voice would not be heard. However, the audience naturally quietened down for Kotetsu-san, as they wanted to hear his voice. By the time I entered sumo, he had already passed away. Due perhaps to letters from fans, his retirement had been delayed, and he had asked to continue for a while because fans would regret his departure.

There were times when I drank too much the previous day. I was uneasy, as I did not know whether I could call out

Chapter 1: Let's Start with Discussion of the Urakata

properly. However, strangely, I performed well when I had a hangover. I don't know why. Generally speaking, in a 15 day tournament, I was satisfied if I could call out to my own standards on just three days.

However, I was always tense, such as when Takanohana was an extremely popular yokozuna. At the time, I was asked whether calling out for a popular rikishi made me tense, however, the matching or rank of those I was calling did not change my feelings. I replied that "It is the same for everyone's bout."

When I first called a yokozuna, I was especially tense. It was when I called Taiho during the jungyo at Ise Shrine. The bouts were held as an elimination tournament, so the yokozuna happened to take part in the first bout, allowing a novice like me to call his name.

Taiho would always stare directly at the yobidashi when his name was called, and we could sense his gaze. This made me especially tense. The same is true of Hakuho. I think he listens very carefully to the voice of the yobidashi.

Further, I also felt tense when the oyakata of my heya, the former Kiyokuni, first sat below the dohyo as a judge. However, I think he was even more tense than I was.

It would not have been acceptable for me to be unable to call out due to a cold, so I always did my best to protect my health. The key to staying healthy is waking up early and going to sleep early.

Some shikona* (sumo names) are easy to call, others are difficult. Everyone else hated "xxnishiki," but I liked it. "Xxkawa" is easy to call. I had difficulty calling "xxyama." It all depends upon the person. There are differences stemming from the number of characters in a name. Names with five syllables are easy to call, while two or three syllables are considered to be difficult. Although he quit early, there was a rikishi with a one syllabled name, Ri. I never called him, but I think his name was difficult. Asashoryu was easy to call, while Asashio and Musoyama were difficult, as was Musashimaru. Calling "ru" constricts one's mouth.

Talking of Musashimaru, there was a time when I was surprised at how well I called his name. I think I was fortunate to have called his name well, but sadly I was not able to comprehend why I had done well and was not able to do so again.

It is difficult to start calling higashi (east) or nishi (west). Personally, I had a preference for nishi. When starting with

Chapter 1: Let's Start with Discussion of the Urakata

higashi, I found myself exhausting my voice calling out "hi-ga-a-shiii..."

There were times when I had thought I had made a mistake, one of which was in the May 2004 tournament, when Asashoryu and Hokutoriki faced off in a playoff for the championship. We only call names once in playoffs. I first called out the higashi rikishi, Asashoryu, then for an instant I found myself at a loss to recall the name of the nishi rikishi, Hokutoriki. I started calling, "Chi...," looking at Kokonoe Oyakata (former Yokozuna Chiyonofuji) who was then the deputy head judge. I immediately realized I was starting to make a mistake, but was able to save the day by looking at the rikishi I was calling, Hokutoriki, and recalling his name.

In the old days, there were amateur yobidashi on jungyo. There were fewer yobidashi at the time, and sometimes these amateurs even helped out in official tournaments. They normally had occupations like farming. There are no foreigners working as yobidashi. Akebono once asked me, "Foreigners can't be yobidashi, can they?" Those who cannot read kanji characters can't be yobidashi. The same applies to Japanese who cannot read kanji properly. In extreme cases, there were even those who had to give up being yobidashi because of their vocal pitch.

The Cheat Sheet Used by Yobidashi

Temochi

Yobidashi have a fan in their right hand when they mount the dohyo, and they also hold a piece of paper in their left hand. This piece of paper is known as "temochi," and is the torikumihyo* (list of bouts) for that day. Yobidashi look at the paper before they go up on the dohyo and thus confirm the names of those in the next bout. I thought it would be sufficient just to remember the names of rikishi I was calling, but as the matches change every day, there are times when I inadvertently forgot the names of the competitors. In such instances, we take a furtive glance at the temochi.

Torikumihyo, or lists of bouts are issued on every day of each tournament. We make enlarged copies of these sheets

Chapter 1: Let's Start with Discussion of the Urakata

and cut and past them division by division, then roll them up as we use them. They are used by the jonokuchi yobidashi onwards, and each yobidashi cuts off his bouts after his time on the dohyo is finished, then hands the sheet to the next yobidashi. The cheat sheet is clean at the beginning, but at the end of the day, there are times when the characters for the rikishi's names are smudged by the sweat of the previous yobidashi. When I became a yobidashi, it was my duty to prepare the cheat sheet. However, because I was the youngest yobidashi, that was the only thing I did.

Taiko——Yaguradaiko and Furedaiko are Important Tasks for the Yobidashi

Taiko (drumming) is indispensable for sumo events. Do-

Yaguradaiko

ing taiko is an important task for the yobidashi. The two main types of taiko are yaguradaiko and furedaiko.

Yaguradaiko is done on top of a high wooden tower. We performed taiko at a rapid tempo on top of a wooden tower constructed high above the place where the sumo performance was held. This drumming consists of yosedaiko and hanedaiko, and is performed between 8:30 and 9:00 a.m., every morning during official tournaments. Yosedaiko is intended to indicate that sumo is being held and urges people to come and watch. In the early years of the Showa Era (1926-1989), yosedaiko was performed early in the morning, but since many people were still asleep, resulting in complaints, it was switched to its present time. Hanedaiko is done at the end of the day, coinciding with the end of the yumitorishiki*, at which time the yobidashi use their wooden clappers to indicate that the performance is over. It is intended to urge people to come again the next day. Hanedaiko has a "ten ten bara bara" tone and is said to reflect people leaving. That's why there is no hanedaiko at the end of the program on the last day of official tournaments, or at other performances which are for only one day.

The yagura*, or wooden tower is quite high at about

Chapter 1: Let's Start with Discussion of the Urakata

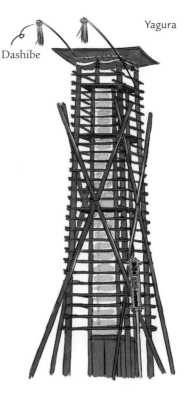

Yagura

Dashibe

16 meters. The taiko is pulled up by rope, and there have been times when it has fallen midway and been broken. But I never did this. An elevator was installed in the tower at Ryogoku Kokugikan from May 1995, making things easier. At official tournaments outside Tokyo, the wooden tower is constructed in a way appropriate for the location. The wooden tower at the Nagoya Basho is high and frightening. No yagura are constructed on jungyo, and taiko is done out in the open.

Above the wooden tower, there are two bamboo poles, which stick out like antennas. These are called dashibe (or dashippei) and symbolize gratitude to heaven. The tips of the poles are tied with hemp and paper streamers.

Furedaiko is done by the yobidashi on the day before the first day, and is intended to tell everyone that sumo begins tomorrow. The yobidashi walk around in the streets while drumming. At the end of the dohyo matsuri*, which I will discuss later, two drums are carried in from the higashi hanamichi* (passage to the dohyo) towards the dohyo. Four yobidashi form a group for each taiko, one man drums, while another taps on the shell of taiko, and they make three circuits around the dohyo, moving leftwards. After they exit out into the open, usually about six yobidashi walk around in the streets. They then proceed to visit each

Furedaiko

Chapter 1: Let's Start with Discussion of the Urakata

heya, as well as patrons. The yobidashi call out, "Sumo wa myonichi ga shonichi jazoe," (tomorrow is the first day of the tournament), "xxumi ni xxyama jazoe." (xxumi vies with xxyama). These are the names of the rikishi who will be competing in the bouts between makuuchi rikishi on the first day. The yobidashi then say, "Goyudan dewa tsumarimasuzoe," meaning, seats are going quickly and will soon be gone. The groups of yobidashi first head to the famous Dewanoumi Beya. This is fixed for 10:00 a.m. However, starting at 10:00 a.m. would possibly result in the yobidashi not being able to reach all the heya during the day, so sometimes this means going to other heya earlier in the morning and reaching Dewanoumi Beya at 10:00 a.m.

If one wants to be in the groups going around doing furedaiko, it is necessary to wait for a vacancy among the existing teams.

I liked furedaiko. I trained my voice for it. Therefore, even after I became the tate yobidashi, I conducted furedaiko training sessions for the young yobidashi. Training is also needed for drumming, and without it one forgets the proper way to do it. Training for everything is important.

Incidentally, there are no music notes for taiko. We learn

everything from our own ears.

Constructing the Dohyo
—— Manual Labor by All the Yobidashi

The construction of the dohyo, or sumo ring, on which the rikishi compete, is called dohyotsuki, and is the job of the yobidashi. The dohyo comprises not only the trapezoid-shaped ring made of dirt, but also the hanging roof above. The circular part of the trapezoid is the actual dohyo where bouts are staged, and the construction of the dohyo encompasses the entire trapezoid. Each side of the trapezoid is 6 meters and 70 centimeters long, with the height ranging between 34 centimeters and 60 centimeters. The ring where bouts are staged has a diameter of 4.55 meters.

The construction of the dohyo is handled by all the yobidashi over a period of three days before each official tournament. To ensure the appropriate dryness of the dirt, as well as other factors, three days is necessary for the construction. In the case of Ryogoku Kokugikan, up to 20 centimeters of the dirt of the old dohyo is removed and rebuilt. The dirt used for this is called Arakida. Clay-like dirt was freshly gathered from a place on the Sumida River, hence the name

Chapter 1: Let's Start with Discussion of the Urakata

Tools used to construct the dohyo.

used for the dirt. Nowadays, however, due to development in the area, dirt from Abiko-shi in Chiba-ken or around Tsukuba in Ibaraki-ken is used instead. About eight tons of this dirt is used in the construction of the dohyo.

First, a hoe is used to dig way the old dirt, with new dirt

put in place and shaped. Crop marks are then used to level and smooth out the surface. A tool called tako is used to harden the surface. Further hardening is done by tataki, or bashing, until the surface becomes tidy. The surface must be sufficiently hard to not leave footprints when heavy rikishi stamp their feet on the dohyo.

Small straw bales, which are used to form the circle on the dohyo, are made at the same time. Straw bags are filled with dirt, and tied with straw rope, with a diameter of about 15 centimeters. The length of the bales differs according to where they are to be used. Those which encompass the ring where the bouts are held are the largest at about 78 centimeters. Sixty-six small bales are used in the construction of the dohyo. The cross-section of the small bales is teardrop shaped and not perfectly circular. To achieve this shape, the small bales are beaten with beer bottles. Being able to make the dohyo properly for official tournaments requires 10 years of experience.

Constructing the dohyo is done completely with human labor.

Once the preparation of the dirt is completed, a spike is placed in the center of the dohyo to serve as an axis, and

Chapter 1: Let's Start with Discussion of the Urakata

a compass is used to draw the circle of the inner dohyo. Grooves are then dug in the line which marks the circle, and small bales are placed there. Rammers are used to solidify the surrounding dirt. Six tenths of the small bales are buried in dirt, with four tenths protruding. This is all that is involved; gigantic rikishi clash on this surface, stamp their feet there, and brace their legs, but the dohyo remains firm. It is quite a mystery. Once a tokudawara*, or special bale, which I will explain later, came off during an official tournament. It had not been fitted well.

Twenty small bales are used for the actual dohyo (inner dohyo) where bouts take place. Of these, four are called tokudawara, which protrude out by one bale in each of four places on the actual dohyo; shomen*, mukojomen*, higashi, and nishi, respectively. The parts of the tokudawara which are above the surface of the dohyo are somewhat larger than the ordinary bales. The reason why these special bales are used is that sumo performances were held outdoors long ago, and when there was rain, it was necessary to drain the water off the dohyo, hence part of the circular dohyo was made to protrude. These protrusions give the rikishi an advantage, and hence are called tokudawara, with toku meaning "advantage" in Japanese.

In addition to the small bales, there are four kakudawara (bales forming the outer rim of the dohyo) on the four sides outside the inner dohyo. Agedawara are placed in all four corners, while fumidawara (bales forming the steps to ascend to the dohyo) are placed. And below the akabusa (red tassel hung above the southeastern corner of the dohyo) and shirobusa (white tassel hung above the southwestern corner), mizuokedawara bales are placed where the water pails are situated. As for the words akabusa and shirobusa, they refer to the tassels hanging below the four corners of the tsuriyane (hanging roof over the ring). These four tassels are aobusa on the east part of the shomen side, kurobusa on the west part of the same side, akabusa on the east part of the mukojomen side, and shirobusa on the west part of the same side. These represent the four seasons and the four gods which rule over them, with ao (blue) representing spring and the Blue Dragon god, aka (red) representing summer and the Red Phoenix god, shiro (white) representing fall and the White Tiger god, and kuro (black) representing winter and the Black Tortoise god.

There are shikiri sen, lines in the middle of the dohyo,

Chapter 1: Let's Start with Discussion of the Urakata

where the rikishi face off. They are white lines 90 centimeters long and 6 centimeters wide. These lines are drawn not only during the construction of the dohyo, but also after the final bout each day during official tournaments, at which time the yobidashi redraw the line. The distance between the east and west shikiri lines is 70 centimeters. The two rikishi competing in a bout perform the shikiri behind this line, and are not allowed to put their hands in front of their own shikiri sen. Shikiri lines were introduced in January 1928. There was nothing dividing the rikishi before that time, with everything left to the two competitors. The shikiri line is enameled and can slip if sand falls on top of it. Therefore, other materials have apparently been tested, but it is still difficult to determine which one is best.

Sand accumulates in a 25 centimeter area outside the small bales of the circular-shaped inner dohyo. This is called janome. Please look at the area around the inner dohyo on television or at the Kokugikan. You will notice that its color is slightly different from other areas outside the inner ring.

Fierce struggles often take place on the edge of the dohyo. Even when rikishi are attacked, they can put their feet on the small bales, and hold out that way. They can even have their heels outside the small bales, as long as they are in midair. However, if they touch the surface outside the bales, the rikishi loses the bout. In such struggles, the sand needs to be arranged to allow footprints to remain. It is duty of the yobidashi to sweep the sand carefully between bouts to ensure that footprints remain.

Rikishi normally try to avoid leaving their footprints in the janome. Young recruits who start their careers from maezumo* after graduating from junior high or high school are taught this in their heya, and learn it properly, however, collegians become rikishi without being so instructed, and some of them leave their footprints in the janome when they throw salt. This is a bit unfortunate, and instruction in this area must be provided. In such cases, the yobidashi sweep the dohyo. Yobidashi in charge of bouts must look closely at the movements of the rikishi, and need to sweep the dohyo whenever the rikishi leave their footprints. In maezumo and other low levels, as the intervals between bouts and the time limit are so short, the yobidashi crouch at the four corners of the dohyo, to be ready to sweep the dohyo immediately.

The yobidashi are also in charge of constructing the dohyo in places other than Ryogoku Kokugikan, such as of-

Chapter 1: Let's Start with Discussion of the Urakata

ficial tournaments outside Tokyo and places where jungyo are held. The only site of an official tournament with a permanent dohyo is the Kokugikan. The dohyo for the official tournaments in Osaka, Nagoya, and Fukuoka is constructed whenever it is needed, with the dirt sourced locally. The dirt used for the Osaka Basho is very good. The stickiness and other attributes of the dirt vary from place to place. Although professionals are tasked with transporting the dirt in most places, sometimes the local soil is unsuitable, such as when it has cement mixed in. When this happens, it hardens quickly, and must be put into the bales the same day. Constructing the dohyo is manual labor. Even though all the yobidashi take part in the work, some of them are elderly. Therefore, the work that requires strenuous physical labor is done by the younger men. When I started as a yobidashi, I lost 10 kilograms from this work.

No yobidashi excel simultaneously in calling out, drumming, and constructing the dohyo. Especially in the case of drumming, very few men can be considered to be really good. There are various ways of drumming. When the bachi (drum sticks) are used parallel to the taiko (drum), it is called hirabachi. I heard Kankichi-san used hirabachi, and he was very good. I was not good at taiko. Since I was so poor at it, I had a good ear for determining who was good at taiko and who was not.

Finally, the dohyo construction manager checks everything, bringing the work to an end, after which the dohyo matsuri can be held. Since official tournaments start on Sunday, the dohyo matsuri takes place from 10:00 a.m. on Saturday, and lasts for about 30 minutes. The ceremony is attended by the rijicho (president of the Sumo Association), the head judge, deputy head judges, and rank-and-file judges, the tate yobidashi, and others. The rikishi ranked in the sanyaku and above also attend. The tate gyoji assumes the role of a shinto priest, and prays for an abundant harvest, peace in the nation, and safety on the dohyo. The yobidashi hit their wooden clappers at times during the ritual. I will omit details for the sake of brevity, but during the dohyo matsuri, sacred items which serve as talismans are buried in a 15 square centimeter hole bored in the center of the dohyo. The items used are dried chestnuts, washed rice, konbu (a type of kelp), dried cuttlefish, salt, and nutmeg. They are put in a kawarake (unglazed earthenware container), wrapped in uncreased Japanese paper, placed in the hole

Chapter 1: Let's Start with Discussion of the Urakata

in the dohyo, and sprinkled with sacred sake. These offerings remain in the dohyo for the entire tournament.

The construction of the dohyo and the dohyo matsuri are open to the public free of charge. Anyone interested should go to watch it. Please call the Nihon Sumo Kyokai to apply. It is also a chance to see the sanyaku rikishi, who attend the dohyo matsuri. Once the rituals are over, the yobidashi carry the taiko to the dohyo, and perform furedaiko as I mentioned earlier.

I will digress a bit here. When I was a sanyaku yobidashi, at the dohyo biraki (the ceremony held on such occasions as the dedication of a new dohyo, when new bales are installed, and when a dohyo is constructed for temporary lodgings at official tournaments outside Tokyo), the officiating priest (gyoji assume the role of a shinto priest during this ceremony) was Tate Gyoji Kimura Shonosuke XXIX of Nishonoseki Beya, whose real name was Sakurai Haruyoshi. At the end of the dohyo matsuri, the tate gyoji utters what is termed "Ametsuchi...," heaven and earth... I consulted with him in advance on this. My words to him were "You will be performing the ceremony at our heya, so would this be inappropriate...?" I then mentioned that the tate gyoji sits on the dohyo and starts speaking after the yobidashi hit their wooden clappers. I thought the use of the clappers at that part of the ritual was meaningless. I suggested that the clappers should instead be used after the tate gyoji had already sat down on the dohyo, as it would be more natural for him to begin the ametsuchi address from there. I asked him, "Wouldn't it be easier to do it this way?" Haruyoshi-san's reply was "Yes, that's a good idea. Let's do it that way from now on." We agreed that it would be done in the new way at my heya's dohyo biraki, and the change was then adopted at official tournaments as well.

In this way, many established routines are decided upon in a random way.

We Have Many Tasks to Fulfill, Including Hitting Wooden Clappers and Carrying Kensho Banners

Hyoshigi, or wooden clappers are also referred as ki. They are made from the wood of cherry trees, and all yobidashi have their own ki. The Yobidashikai (organization of the yobidashi) has two pairs, but everyone is expected to have their own ki. There are differences in sound among

Chapter 1: Let's Start with Discussion of the Urakata

Clappers (ki)

The clapper held in the left hand protrudes a little.

The top of the right clapper should match the middle of the left one.

ki. I was passed down some ki by my elders, however, it is always best to use the ki which one is most familiar with. The ki used in the left hand protrudes a little, while the one for the right hand is set back somewhat, and the top of the right one should match the middle of the left one. This is called ki o ireru or ki ga hairu, and is not referred to as ki o utsu (hitting the ki). I learned this as soon as I first went on jungyo. Anyone can learn to do this with just a little practice. I even taught Hakuho-zeki how to do it. He was able to do it properly, but making a good sound from the ki is another matter. It is difficult to do.

As for when the ki are used, the first time is 30 minutes before the first bout of the day, when the rikishi enter the east and west shitakubeya to await their bouts. This is called the first ki. The second ki is in shitakubeya 15 minutes before the first bout. After the second ki, the rikishi exit from shitakubeya and gather before the hanamichi, and clap their cheeks, move their bodies around, and engage in other preparations. The ki are used again just before the bouts begin; this is referred to as yobiki. After all the bouts are concluded, the ki are used again after the yumitorishiki finishes. This is the time when the day's program comes to an end.

Other than the above, the yobidashi have many other tasks to perform on and around the dohyo. Please watch them and see what they do. These tasks are not shown much on television, however.

First, we need to tell the rikishi when it is time to begin their bout. The judge who serves as the timekeeper looks at his watch and signals us. Almost all rikishi start their bouts at the appointed time, however, they are also allowed to begin their bouts early if they so desire. But if they actually do start the bout early, we have to be prepared to take the necessary steps for this. This can be confusing for us.

Further, approximately 45 kilograms of sea salt, called kiyome no shio (salt for purification), is thrown by rikishi

Chapter 1: Let's Start with Discussion of the Urakata

on the dohyo during a single day in an official tournament. Preparing this salt, handing dippers to the rikishi offering water, going up on the dohyo with a banner to indicate a default win, carrying the prize banners on the dohyo, assisting rikishi who have been injured, are all tasks we must handle. When there are many prize banners, we sometimes need to go back on the dohyo with a second batch of banners.

Cleaning up after cushions have been thrown is also difficult. If a yokozuna losses, cushions are thrown onto the

dohyo. I understand the feelings of the audience, but this practice is prohibited because it is dangerous. Oranges and other objects have also been thrown, and have caused injuries. There was even an instance of a cushion hitting the gyoji handling the public address system, pushing the microphone against his face and injuring him.

Throwing objects once had the meaning of offering congratulations. When a rikishi one supported won, fans used to throw haori (formal Japanese coats) and tobacco pouches, etc. They had the trade names or family crests of the owners imprinted on them, so it was possible to determine who had thrown them, and after the yobidashi had gathered the cushions, the rikishi's tsukebito* could then return them to the owners and receive a congratulatory gift. This custom, called "nagehana" was prohibited in 1909, after which zabuton (cushions) were thrown. Today, cushions that cannot be thrown are used in the Kyushu Basho in November, but in other official tournaments, cushions continue to be thrown. Catching the cushions while they are still flying and putting them back where they belong is a task for the yobidashi. It can be a dangerous and arduous job, and we hope this throwing of cushions can be stopped.

Chapter 1: Let's Start with Discussion of the Urakata

Sweeping the dohyo is an important task and requires know-how. One cannot apply too much strength while sweeping, as this results in all the sand moving. There is a degree of measurement for this which cannot be expressed in words. Having a lot of experience with sweeping enables one to skillfully use the tip of the broom.

In this way, yobidashi have many tasks to handle, during which time they watch many bouts. It is also necessary for yobidashi to watch practice at their heya. All this helps yobidashi understand the flow of sumo. Once they master this, they are able to react quickly, such as by removing the water pail when rikishi fall from the dohyo.

The Daily Life of a Yobidashi——in My Case

When official tournaments or jungyo are held, the yobidashi are fairly busy, but we have free time on other occasions, and in my case, I often went to see movies. I had no problems doing this even when I went out without saying a word.

When I became a yobidashi, I used to wake up at 6:00 a.m. to prepare tea for the oyakata and do cleaning. In the case of official tournaments outside Tokyo, I also needed to fire up the bath and do other tasks. In the Osaka Basho in March, it is still cold, so setting up the baths made me warm and was enjoyable.

The rikishi in the heya do keiko* (practice) in the morning and then have their first meal at lunch. Since yobidashi do not do keiko, we were able to eat breakfast. Isegahama Oyakata's okamisan* (wife) always told me I was welcome to have breakfast in the heya, but I hesitated to do so alone, so I would go out to a coffee shop to have their set breakfast.

After keiko is over, the yobidashi sweep the dohyo. This serves as practice for the same task in official tournaments.

When I entered sumo, Kiyokuni still lived in the heya. About a year later, I recall that he got married and moved out. I had still only just entered sumo. Rikishi ranked in the jumaime and above were on a different plane, so it was very difficult to talk with them. And further, Kiyokuni was an ozeki. I almost never talked to him and it was difficult to get to know him. However, after he retired from active competition, we started to have friendly conversations. When I addressed rikishi, I added zeki to the name of sekitori, while I appended san to the names of the lower-ranked rikishi, or just called them by their nicknames.

Chapter 1: Let's Start with Discussion of the Urakata

Yobidashi and gyoji belong to heya, but they are free to move out to other lodgings if they so desire. Everyone lives together in the same room every day, and if one dislikes such arrangements, they can rent an apartment and commute to the heya. Sometimes, several people rented an apartment together, but I think that made it into the same communal living arrangement as in the heya, but with the additional disadvantage of needing to pay rent. Living in the heya means having almost no living expenses. Some heya charge a little for food and other expenses. In my case, that was 5,000 yen. My initial monthly salary was 15,000 yen, which resulted in me using up my remaining allowance in a single week. However, the heya's charge of 5,000 yen did not change even after my salary increased, and I was able to save money. Instead of renting an apartment, I was able to buy my own house when I was in my 20s, and moved there. Before buying the house, when I told Isegahama Oyakata about this, he asked, "Will you actually buy your own place?" However, he did nothing to prevent me from moving there. He passed away soon after.

After I moved out of the heya, I commuted there, as well as to the Kokugikan. I began to wonder whether I actually needed to go to the heya every day. I continued to do so at first, but I soon started not to go on days when there was nothing to do. Nobody said anything. The number of times I went to the heya gradually decreased. However, there was no problem with this as long as I did the work I was supposed to do properly.

As the tate yobidashi, I went to the official tournaments at about 11:00 a.m. I then changed clothes and drank tea, by which time the morning was over. During official tournaments, I had no tsukebito, but one man was assigned as a caretaker, and brought tea for me and performed other tasks. On jungyo only, I had my own tsukebito from the time I reached jumaime yobidashi status.

We eat bento (boxed meals) at lunchtime, and if there are any visitors, I meet them then, and wait for my own appearance on the dohyo. During official tournaments, I did not need to provide guidance to younger yobidashi. My own task was to just call out the last bout. One has quite a lot of free time as the tate yobidashi.

The Taikozuka——Performing Religious Services for the Souls of Departed Yobidashi

At the back of the Ryogoku Ekoin's (temple) cemetery is

the Taikozuka, a monument which enshrines the souls of generations of deceased yobidashi. The monument was proposed by Yobidashi Hasegawa Kantaro, and was erected in October 1913. Even today, all the yobidashi gather there after the end of every May tournament, to attend a Buddhist memorial service.

The monument to past generations of yobidashi. It is called the Taikozuka.

The memorial may have been intended to hold the remains of some yobidashi who were not able to acquire their own graves. The ashes of some yobidashi who have no surviving relatives are interred in the memorial.

Gyoji——Sumo's Referees-Judging Bouts is Their First Responsibility

Of all the men who play a supporting role in sumo, I

think gyoji are the most conspicuous. They are dressed in beautiful costumes and are on the dohyo together with the rikishi, who play the leading part in sumo, during all bouts. However, this is not the only job the gyoji handle. Like yobidashi, they undertake a variety of tasks in the background.

It goes without saying that the primary role of the gyoji is to referee matches. The yobidashi call the rikishi, and when the latter step on to the dohyo, their work begins. First, the gyoji calls out the names of the rikishi who have stepped on to the dohyo. For bouts between hiramaku* (maegashira*) rikishi, the gyoji calls their names only once, such as xxkawa ni xxyama. If one of the rikishi is in the sanyaku and the other a hiramaku man, the gyoji calls out "Kataya xxkawa, xxkawa, konata xxyama, xxyama," thus calling out the names of both rikishi twice each. For the last bout of the day, the gyoji says, "Kono sumo ichiban nite honjitsu no uchidome." (This is the last bout of the day). In the case of the last bout on the senshuraku* (final day of the tournament), the gyoji includes the words, "Kono sumo ichiban nite senshuraku," which translates as this bout closes the tournament. In the final bout of the jumaime, the gyoji calls out the names of both rikishi twice, as in bouts

Chapter 1: Let's Start with Discussion of the Urakata

between sanyaku rikishi, and adds the words, "Kono sumo ichiban nite nakairi," translating as after this bout, the makuuchi* bouts start after nakairi* (a brief intermission).

After the rikishi step up on the dohyo, the gyoji does a lot of shouting.

When the two rikishi begin their shikiri, he says "Miote." This word means that the rikishi should synchronize their breathing at the tachiai* (initial charge), but some gyoji say "Miatte," "Miawashite," "Kamaete," or "Yudannaku." Both rikishi are supposed to touch both of their hands on the dohyo just before the tachiai, and to urge them to do so, the gyoji will say "Te o oroshite" (put your hands down), and when they do not appear to be ready, he will say "Mada, mada." (or not yet.)

After a number of shikiri, it will be seigen jikan* (time is up). There will have been a signal from the judge who serves as the timekeeper. Seeing this, the gyoji will say "Jikan desu," meaning now is the time to begin the bout, and then "Mattanashi," or no false starts.

The two rikishi rise and clash, beginning the bout, at which time the gyoji will shout "Hakkyoi," and "Nokotta," any number of times depending upon the progress of the bout. He will say "Hakkyoi," to urge the rikishi to rouse themselves when their movement slows or stops. This word originates from hakkiyoyo, which means to rouse oneself. Some gyoji say "Hakkeyoi" or "Hakkiyoi." On the other hand, when the rikishi exchange blows, the gyoji will shout repeatedly, "Nokotta, nokotta."

During the bout, the gyoji will constantly move around. While the rikishi are almost naked, the gyoji have a costume wrapped around them, which is especially trying in the summer, as they must keep moving around the dohyo in synch with the fierce battle between the two rikishi. If the gyoji's movements are slow, he will be hit by the rikishi and become an obstacle to the bout, and possibly be in danger of being injured himself. Actually, some gyoji have been thrown over. However, this is not the only reason why gyoji keep moving. There is also a policy that they must not stay in one place, but need to be in motion so as not to become an obstacle to the view of the judges and audience.

When the bout drags on with both rikishi showing signs of tiring, a mizuiri (water break) is called. The standard for this is when the bout has been running for four or five minutes. Once this amount of time has elapsed, the judge serv-

Chapter 1: Let's Start with Discussion of the Urakata

ing as timekeeper will signal to the gyoji. The gyoji will then get confirmation from the judges and interrupt the bout. This is a mizuiri. The rikishi temporarily step down from the dohyo, take chikaramizu* (literally "water of power"), while their mawashi*, which have become loose, are tightened. Once this is all done, they will have a brief break. The rikishi will then return to the dohyo, resume the same position they were in when the bout was interrupted, with the gyoji restoring their grips based on memory. The gyoji will then confirm that there are no objections from the rikishi or judges. At this moment the gyoji will shout "Iika, iika" (Is this alright?), and simultaneously tap the mawashi of both rikishi. In this way, the bout is resumed.

If the bout is still not decided, one more mizuiri can be called. If there is then still no winner, a rematch will be held two bouts later, with the rikishi having a break during that time. When there is a rematch, the two rikishi will start from the shikiri again.

Gunbai——Essential Item for Gyoji

During the time they are on the dohyo, gyoji always carry their gunbai. It is indispensable for a gyoji's work. It is

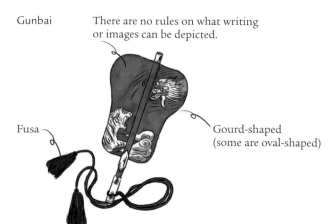

Gunbai — There are no rules on what writing or images can be depicted.

Fusa

Gourd-shaped (some are oval-shaped)

made from keyaki (Japanese zelkova), kashi (evergreen oak), shitan (rosewood), or other woods, and coated with lacquer, and has writing or images inscribed on it. There are actually no restrictions on what can be depicted on the gunbai. There are many different types of inscriptions. The tassel and string part of the gunbai is called the gunbai no fusa. Some gunbai are handed down from previous generations, and are known as yuzuri uchiwa.

Gyoji use their gunbai to declare the winners of bouts, and there is an expression related to this. Once time is up, both rikishi enter into their final shikiri, and the gyoji raises

Chapter 1: Let's Start with Discussion of the Urakata

his wrist and turns his gunbai towards himself. At this point, with it pointing down, the gunbai's surface can be seen, and this is referred to as "gunbai o kaesu," or in other words the gyoji is signalling the imminent start of a bout. The gyoji says "Jikan desu" (it is time) to the rikishi, and then "Mattanashi," or "Matta arimasen" (both of these being exhortations to have no false starts). The rikishi then synchronize themselves at the tachiai, at which moment the gyoji pulls his gunbai back towards himself. This is known as "gunbai o hiku."

Once the bout is decided, the gyoji points his gunbai in the direction of the winner, either on the east side or west side. This is known as "gunbai o ageru." No matter how difficult it may be to determine the winner, the gyoji is required to immediately point his gunbai in the direction of the winner. He cannot look aside. If the bout is decided, the gyoji points his gunbai in the direction of the winner and calls out his name. For the winning rikishi, this is called gunbai o ukeru, and makes him officially the winner. However, in the case of a monoii, even if the gunbai has been pointed at him, the rikishi cannot claim to have been declared the winner.

A monoii, or challenge of the gyoji's decision occurs when

the shimpan, or judges, object to the verdict of the gyoji. A monoii is called when one of the judges raises his hand. All the judges come up on to the dohyo to confer. The result can be that the gyoji's verdict is upheld, overturned, or a rematch is called because the bout was too close. The shimpancho, or head judge explains the decision on the public address system. If a rematch has been called, the bout is then repeated, and if the decision has been upheld or reversed, the winning rikishi finally receives the gunbai pointed in his direction. Rikishi waiting below the dohyo are also permitted to call a monoii, however, they cannot participate in the discussion. The gyoji participates in the discussion by the shimpan on the dohyo, however, he cannot raise any objections, even if he disagrees with the verdict of the judges.

When a decision is challenged and the judges confer, the rikishi get down from the dohyo. In such cases, the rikishi often ask the yobidashi, "What do you think." We would never say "You lost," so it is difficult to reply. We typically say "I don't know," or "There needs to be a rematch." If we are really sure that the rikishi asking us actually won, we might say, "You won." When a gyoji's decision is overturned (sashichigae), in other words an error on the part of the gyo-

Chapter 1: Let's Start with Discussion of the Urakata

ji, it is commonly referred to as a "gyoji kuroboshi," or a loss for the gyoji. When a tate gyoji has his decision overturned, he offers his resignation to the rijicho the same day. Absolute accuracy is not actually required of the gyoji, but given that bouts can be decided in a split-second, it is a very demanding profession. The tate gyoji have a short sword on their waist. This symbolizes that they are ready to disembowel themselves if the decision is overturned. Of course no gyoji has ever actually done so.

The tanto, or short sword, worn by gyoji is not real, and it is likely to be made from bamboo. However, when Abe Masao-san became Kimura Shonosuke XXXI, he told me the short sword was real. Undoubtedly the sword was designed so that it could not cut.

After the bout is decided, if there is a prize to be awarded, the gyoji will give it to the winning rikishi after placing it on his gunbai.

Gyoji Handle the Public Address System

Everyone listens to the public address system without giving it much thought. I think most people believe that the Nihon Sumo Kyokai has people specially trained to handle the public address system, but such is not the case. The announcements, such as "Higashi kata, xxyama, from xx, belong to xx beya, the gyoji is xxxx," and later, "Tadaima no kimarite* wa oshidashi, oshidashi de xxyama no kachi," or the bout was won by oshidashi, xxyama won by oshidashi, are all made by gyoji. They do not wear their costumes for this work, and instead use business suits and ties, and thus many people do not realize that they are gyoji.

As to where the announcements are made from; there is a simple table is in the boxed seat closest to the dohyo. No special booth or enclosure is used. The announcements are made by a team of two gyoji. This role is handled by makuuchi gyoji, jumaime gyoji, and makushita gyoji. One of the gyoji handling the announcements looks at the dohyo, while the other fixes his eyes on a monitor. This allows him to confirm the winning technique and announce it properly. There is a short interval between the end of the bout and the announcement of the winning technique. If there is difficulty in determining the winning technique, the gyoji will consult with the four or five oyakata, called kimarite gakari, who monitor bouts in the video room, then announce the appropriate technique. Sometimes there is

Chapter 1: Let's Start with Discussion of the Urakata

quite an interval between the end of the bout and the announcement of the technique, and this is to facilitate consultation. The gyoji handling the announcements also comes to the side of the dohyo during the dohyoiri*, and introduces the rikishi. Some people are more suited to this work than others, and those with high-pitched voices are not suitable.

Kimura Shonosuke XXVIII was in charge of the public address system for a lengthy period of time and thus learned much about it. He also handled the Sumo Kyokai's official funeral for my master, Terukuni-san. He was a great man.

Kimura Shonosuke XXXII, whose real name is Sawada Ikuya, had an excellent style and his voice when he was handling the public address system was also very good. This man was good at everything, but he did not really want to take on these tasks, so when he was praised, he would invariably say "You must be joking." If I would say "Please do it because you are so good," he would say "What are you talking about?" When this man retired, Dewanoumi Oyakata (ex-Washuyama), who operated the heya to which he belonged, told him to bow his head and show humility at his farewell party, even if just that once. I have heard that was how he was able to be given a retirement ceremony party. His calligraphy was also outstanding, but it was very difficult to get him to write anything. He would simply say, "I don't do that kind of thing."

Presenting the Kaobure
—— Done by the Gyoji and Yobidashi

Presenting the kaobure, or sheets listing the next day's bouts, is the responsibility of the gyoji. Following the yokozuna dohyoiri*, one of the tate gyoji presents the next day's makuuchi bouts. This is not done on the final day, of course, as there are no bouts on the next day. Sometimes, due to the progress of bouts on that day, time may be lim-

Reading out the next day's bouts

Chapter 1: Let's Start with Discussion of the Urakata

ited, and it is up to the gyoji to decide whether to omit the ceremony.

Yobidashi are also involved in the presentation of the kaobure, and I will describe this in detail. The gyoji and yobidashi step up on to the dohyo with the kaobure. The kaobure are sheets of paper 48 centimeters high and 33 centimeters wide, on which the gyoji have written the matchings for the next day's bouts in sumi (India ink). The gyoji's first words as he starts reading the matchings are "Habakarinagara, myonichi no torikumi o gohiro tsukamatsurimasu," meaning with all due respect, we announce tomorrow's bouts. The gyoji then places the kaobure on top of a white fan in his left hand, reads the matchings, such as "xxxyama niwa xxxkawa," after which they are turned in the higashi, shomen, nishi, and mukojomen directions. A yobidashi crouches by the gyoji, takes each sheet by his left hand, shows it to the nishi and mukojomen sides, then changes it over to his right hand and displays it to the higashi and mukojomen sides. This is repeated until all the next day's bouts are read, after which the gyoji concludes by saying, "Migi aitsutomemasuru aida, myonichi mo niginigishiku goraijo o machi tatematsurimasu." About seven minutes is required to complete this ceremony. During this time, the yobidashi has to continue crouching. While not to the level of rikishi, the yobidashi need strong legs and loins to do so this. As I have strong legs and loins, this was never a problem for me, but some men need to persevere with quivering legs. The yobidashi also has to hold up the increasing number of kaobure until the end, and this makes one's arms tired. Further, holding the kaobure tightly results in the yobidashi having to touch the India ink on the sheets, which may mix with the sweet on his palms, which become soiled by the ink.

Kimura Masanao III, who became Shikimori Inosuke XXIV, read the kaobure slowly, and working with him could be tiring.

The Banzuke is Written in Sumoji

The banzukehyo, commonly referred to as the banzuke, is issued each tournament and lists, packed in closely on a single page, all the rikishi, gyoji, toshiyori*, wakaimonogashira, sewanin, yobidashi in jumaime and above, and the tokoyama. It is centered on the rikishi, who are divided into the higashi (east) and nishi (west) sides, starting with the yokozuna, ozeki, sekiwake, and komusubi*, with larger, thicker

Chapter 1: Let's Start with Discussion of the Urakata

writing the higher the rikishi is. Writing this is the responsibility of the gyoji. They write it on a sheet of Kent paper, 110 centimeters high and 80 centimeters wide. Frame lines are first drawn with a pencil, then the inscription is done with a writing brush. About three gyoji work together on the banzuke. When I first entered sumo, I helped a gyoji in my heya draw the lines on the banzuke.

The banzuke is divided into the higashi and nishi sides, with "gomenkomuru" written in large characters in the middle. These words are vestiges of the Edo Era, when permission from the shogunate office responsible for the management of temples and shrines was needed to hold kanjin-zumo at such places. The dates of the tournament are inscribed below and where it will be held, then the names of the gyoji, and finally the names of the shimpan (judges). There are five levels, and on the left edge at the bottom, "konohoka chu maezumo tozai ni gozasoro," "senshu banzai daidai kano" are written. The meaning of the earlier expression is that, in addition to the names listed on the banzuke, there are also rikishi in honchu and maezumo. Maezumo are rikishi who have just entered sumo, while honchu, now defunct, was a rank between jonokuchi* and maezumo. The latter expression means "to have a full house for one thousand years and for ten thousand years."

Once the writing has been completed, the banzuke is printed at a reduced size of 58 centimeters high and 44 centimeters wide, with 600,000 copies printed each tournament. Since writing the banzuke takes a number of days, the gyoji in charge does not go on jungyo, and instead concentrates on the banzuke. The gyoji are extremely careful when they write the banzuke, and there are very seldom mistakes. However, many years ago, there was a case of a rikishi from Hokkaido who was mistakenly listed as being from Aomori. The entire banzuke does not need to be rewritten when there is a mistake; errors are corrected by pasting paper over them and rewriting.

The brush writing is done in sumoji style, which is unique to sumo. One of the key points of this style is that the gaps between characters are kept to the minimum, as this is supposed to be an omen that there will be a full house of patrons. Gyoji start learning this work when they are trainees, and some turn out to be proficient, while others are not. Those who write the banzuke have reached a certain level of proficiency, but just being able to write characters well does not necessarily mean that one can write sumoji well.

Recording the results of bouts is done by the gyoji. A long scroll about 90 meters long, called the maki, lists all rikishi from yokozuna down to the jonokuchi in the order they appear on the banzuke. This is written by the gyoji, using sumoji, and each day's results are added to the scroll. If a rikishi loses a bout, a stamp with his name is placed above the winning rikishi's name, and if he wins a bout, the stamp with the name of his opponent is placed below his name.

In addition to the above, the gyoji act as record keepers at the banzuke formulation conference. They have many tasks which involve writing. And there was a gyoji in my heya who started writing as soon as he woke up in the morning. He did this without being told to do so. They can never be idle in the heya. Gyoji handle office work in their heya, such as addressing envelopes for important ceremonial occasions.

Gyoji Wear Different Costumes According to Their Rank

Gyoji also have ranks, with eight levels, starting with jonokuchi gyoji, jonidan gyoji, sandanme gyoji, makushita gyoji, jumaime gyoji, makuuchi gyoji, sanyaku gyoji, and finally the highest rank of tate gyoji. Sometimes, all gyoji at the makushita level and below are collectively referred to as makushita gyoji ika.

There are two tate gyoji, named Kimura Shonosuke and Shikimori Inosuke. Kimura Shonosuke only handles the final bout. Gyoji in jumaime and above handle two bouts each, however, formally speaking, there is flexibility in this area.

All gyoji use either the Kimura or Shikimori names. Therefore they are all either Kimura-san or Shikimori-san, and for this reason people in the sumo world are seldom

Chapter 1: Let's Start with Discussion of the Urakata

called by their surnames. If we were just to say Kimura-san, nobody would know whom we were referring to. And yobidashi do not even use surnames.

Although yobidashi of all ranks wear the same attire, in the case of gyoji, their clothing as well as the color of the tassels on the gunbai differs according to their rank. All the gyoji wear hitatare, or ancient ceremonial court robes, eboshi*, or black-lacquered caps and have a gunbai. The kikutoji, or flower-shaped objects on their breasts, sleeves, and cuffs are all of the same color as the tassels on the gunbai. As for the differences in appearance according to rank, the tate gyoji have a short sword on their left side, and an inro, or seal case dangling from their right side. They also wear white tabi (Japanese socks) and indoor sandals. The two tate gyoji use different colors on their tassels; Kimura Shonosuke uses dark purple, while Shikimori Inosuke has purple and white. Sanyaku gyoji and below do not have short swords, sanyaku gyoji have inro, white tabi, and indoor sandals, while the color of the tassels on their gunbai is vermillion. Makuuchi gyoji do not have either inro or indoor sandals, while they have red and white tassels on their gunbai, and use white tabi. Jumaime gyoji have blue and white tassels on their gunbai and use white tabi, while gyoji in the makushita and below have black or blue tassels on their gunbai and are bare-footed. Detecting the differences in costume between the gyoji, either by going to the Kokugikan from an early hour, or by watching television, is one of the ways to enjoy sumo.

The Tokoyama's Work——They Become Full-Fledged When They Can Arrange Oichomage

Tokoyama arrange the hair of rikishi. Like gyoji and yobidashi, they belong to heya, and arrange the hair of the rikishi of the heya to which they belong. There is a three year apprenticeship period, during which they are sent to study in heya with experienced senior tokoyama, as assigned by the Nihon Sumo Kyokai.

There are two types of topknots, ordinary mage and oichomage*. The oichomage on the front of the rikishi's head resembles the leaf of an icho (ginkgo tree), and is hence called an

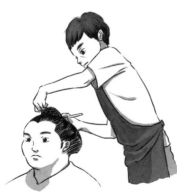

Tokoyama arranging oichomage

Chapter 1: Let's Start with Discussion of the Urakata

oicho. Rikishi ranked in the jumaime and above, in other words, sekitori, use oichomage. Further, rikishi ranked in the makushita have oichomage when they are matched with opponents ranked in the jumaime and above, as a gesture of respect. Rikishi who perform the yumitorishiki and shokiri (or shokkiri), both of which I will describe later, have oichomage even though they are not sekitori.

However, sekitori do not always have their hair arranged in an oichomage. Other than for their bouts during tournaments and on other formal occasions, they have an ordinary topknot.

Tokoyama can be termed full-fledged when they can arrange oichomage. From what I saw, it takes a minimum of about five years for them to reach this level. As for the average amount of time needed to arrange a rikishi's oichomage, even a proficient tokoyama will require 20 to 30 minutes.

When I entered sumo, Isegahama Beya had two tokoyama, one of whom commuted from his home. When they make their debut, tokoyama start work early in the morning, but as their rank becomes higher, they can wake up later, as they have no work in the early hours. After rikishi finish their morning keiko, and return from their baths, the tokoyama's work begins. After Kiyokuni became ozeki, he had his hair arranged before keiko, so the tokoyama had to wake up early. Tokoyama only need to arrange the topknots of the rikishi. Yobidashi are free after their work is completed, however, tokoyama must often synchronize their schedules with those of the sekitori, so in reality they may not have much free time.

Tokoyama also have a ranking system, which starts from goto, or fifth class and goes up to tokuto, or special class. Although their work is centered around arranging hair, they do not need qualifications such as those of hairdressers or beauticians. However, there were some men with a hairdresser's license.

The tools used by the tokoyama are combs such as aragushi, maekaki, and sukigushi, as well as nigiribasami and kamisori. They also need magebo for when they are arranging an oichomage, and yasuri. They require natane abura (rapeseed oil), and suki abura (oil), called bintsuke abura, the main ingredient of which is from mokuro from Kyushu, made from hazenomi (wax tree fruit), for glazing. The distinctive fragrance that rikishi have is derived from this. Further, paper cords, or motoyui, are necessary. These consist of strips of robust washi (Japanese paper) wrapped in cotton, and are then coated with paste made from seaweed and rice, and dried. These cords are used to tie the hair of the rikishi. Sometimes the cords come off during fierce bouts, but tokoyama are not responsible for this.

Former Rikishi Become Wakaimonogashira and Sewanin

Wakaimonogashira are often simply called "kashira." They are members of the Nihon Sumo Kyokai, belong to a heya, and provide supervision, educational guidance, and other help to trainee rikishi who have passed the physical examination (or rikishi in the lower divisions). They also maintain the record of the results of bouts and monitor their progress, in addition to assisting rikishi who have been injured or are ill.

All of these men are former rikishi. They retired from active competition in the jumaime or makushita and were considered qualified for the position. The maximum number of wakaimonogashira is set at eight.

The qualifications for becoming a sewanin are the same as those for wakaimonogashira, and though there were originally a maximum of eight, that has now increased. Sewanin assist wakaimonogashira in their duties, and their mission is to safekeep and transport the equipment needed for sumo. Setting up tents on jungyo is also the responsibility of the sewanin. They also work at the kido (ticket gate) and converse with fans there. Further, the sewanin also manage shitakubeya.

Shitakubeya is the waiting room (or changing room) for rikishi, and is formally called rikishi hikaeshitsu in Japanese. Rikishi assemble there before their bouts, put on their mawashi, and do warm-up exercises, relax, and think of how they will make their tachiai. At the Kokugikan, shitakubeya are situated at the back of the hanamichi of both the east and west sides, but rikishi ranked on the east and west sides of the banzuke do not necessary use the respective east and west shitakubeya. For example, rikishi who are competing against a lower ranked opponent use the shitakubeya on their own side of the banzuke, while rikishi facing a higher ranked rival go to the side opposite of that of their opponent.

Wakaimonogashira and sewanin continue to use the name they had while they were active rikishi.

Chapter 2

Sumo's Leading Actors- Rikishi and Oyakata

What is Needed to Become a Rikishi

Men who have passed the Nihon Sumo Kyokai's physical examination and have been registered are called rikishi. The physical examination for new rikishi is popularly known as the shindeshi* kensa, and is held a few days before the first day of every official tournament.

To be eligible to take the shindeshi kensa, a prospective recruit must have completed compulsory school education, and must also be less than 23 years of age. However, men who have respectable records in tournaments, designated by the Nihon Sumo Kyokai, for working adults or amateurs,

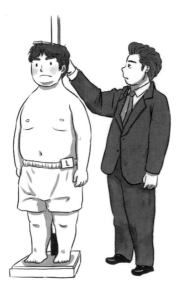

may apply until they turn 25. There are also physical requirements; recruits must stand at 167 centimeters and above and weigh at least 67 kilograms. In the case of the Osaka Basho in March, those who are about to graduate from junior high school are accepted if they stand at 165

Chapter 2: Sumo's Leading Actors-Rikishi and Oyakata

centimeters or higher.

Those who satisfy the above requirements can take the shindeshi kensa. To apply for the physical, the applicant must have the master of the heya he wishes to join submit application forms for him to the Nihon Sumo Kyokai, and if he passes the physical administered by a physician designed by the Kyokai, he can then become a rikishi. The highest number of applicants is in the March tournament, which coincides with the time students graduate from schools.

Those recruits who pass the examination compete in maezumo, which begins on the third day of all tournaments, except for March, when it starts on the second day. Maezumo is also called banzuke-gai (off the banzuke), as rikishi at that level have still not been ranked. Rikishi continue competing until they win three bouts, and are promoted in the order in which they achieve this. They then appear in the shinjo shusse hiro (the ceremony to introduce new recruits on the dohyo), and their names will be listed in the jonokuchi on the banzuke for the next tournament.

A gyoji at makushita level or below speaks at the shinjo shusse hiro. In this ceremony, all the rikishi who have become shinjo get up on the dohyo together, and the gyoji says, "Tozai tozai, kore ni hikaeorimasu, rikishigi ni gozarimasu. Tadaima made wa banzuke-gai ni toraseokimashita tokoro, tobasho hibi seiseki yushu ni tsuki, honjitsu yori banzuke-men ni sashikuwaeokimasuru aida, igo aikawarazu gohiiki ohikitate no hodo, hitoe ni negaiage tate matsurimasu." (East and west, east and west, please take note of this ceremony for these rikishi. Until now, they were in banzuke-gai, however, by achieving good records in this tournament, they will henceforth be listed on the banzuke, and we respectfully request that you continue to support them). The new rikishi wear keshomawashi*, but as they still have not had their own ones made, they borrow those of senior rikishi.

Once they become shinjo, the new rikishi study in the Sumo Kyoshujo (sumo school) for six months. The Sumo Kyoshujo was established in 1957 and is situated within Ryogoku Kokugikan. They study practical sumo skills and are given lectures in various educational subjects. Practical sumo skills are taught by oyakata who are Kyoshujo instructors as well as by active rikishi, and include basic exercises such as shiko* (leg raising and stomping), teppo* (striking a pole), and suriashi* (sliding feet). Shiko is an often

Chapter 2: Sumo's Leading Actors-Rikishi and Oyakata

seen sumo exercise; the rikishi raises one leg and thumps it down. Teppo is a form of training for tsuppari (thrusting). Holding his left arm firmly in place, the rikishi thrusts with his right hand to his side and simultaneously does suriashi with his right foot. This is repeated on the left and right sides and is the key movement for one's hands and feet when attacking. In the keikoba* of sumo beya* there is a pillar, called a teppobashira, for this purpose.

Shiko

Suriashi

Teppo

Shiko and teppo are among the most basic fundamentals of sumo. There is a saying that "Shiko is juryo and teppo is makuuchi." This means that doing shiko properly is appropriate for a juryo (jumaime) rikishi, and doing teppo well makes a makuuchi rikishi. Suriashi is going around the dohyo without stepping out.

The educational courses include the history of sumo, Japanese (including calligraphy), social studies, sumo jinku (songs), and sports medicine. Practical sumo skills are taught in the morning from Monday to Friday, after which there is an educational lecture for about an hour. After the lecture, the rikishi take a bath, have lunch, clean up, and then leave. The educational classes are also open to gyoji, yobidashi, and other people in the Nihon Sumo Kyokai, if they wish to attend.

Food, clothing, and shelter are all provided by the heya to which one belongs. Thus the recruits do not starve. Further, the Nihon Sumo Kyokai provides an allowance each tournament, so young rikishi have at least a small amount of pocket money. Some heya retain a portion of this allowance as savings.

Even shindeshi are expected to dress in an appropriate

Chapter 2: Sumo's Leading Actors-Rikishi and Oyakata

fashion for rikishi when they go out. In the summer, this is a yukata, and when it gets colder, a kimono. They do not need to dress in this fashion when they are in the heya; all wear T-shirts and sweaters in the heya. They can wear sweaters and the like when they only go a short distance outside, such as to a convenience store.

The number of foreign rikishi is now increasing, and there is an especially large number of Mongolians. The Mongolians are the most close-knit; they get together and advise each other. I think this is a good thing. Many foreign rikishi are not able to become accustomed to sumo and leave. Foreign rikishi have difficulty especially when they enter sumo. Takasago Beya, to which Takamiyama belonged, was strict, and it was very difficult for him at first. The Takasago Oyakata of the time was ex-Yokozuna Maedayama. I have heard that Takamiyama went around and around on the Yamanote Line, and cried, as he did not have

the money to return to Hawaii, and as he had handed over his passport. However, he persevered, and achieved great success. His okamisan was a very good person and was very patient and supportive; as he was not familiar with the taste of chanko*, she would make ham and eggs for him.

The Promotion of Rikishi
—— Those Who Reach Jumaime are Called Sekitori

How are rikishi promoted?

Rikishi who are promoted from banzuke-gai to jonokuchi are listed on the banzuke in very small writing. As there are sometimes a total of up to 100 men in the division, it is necessary that their names be written in very small characters on the banzuke. Since the names are so difficult to discern, they are called mushimegane (magnifying glass), which one literally needs to read the characters. When someone starts on something, the expression "I am still in the jonokuchi," derives from sumo.

Above the jonokuchi comes the jonidan*, and it is said that the name of the division is derived from it being the second lowest level on the banzuke. The names written in the third level on the banzuke from the top are those of the

Chapter 2: Sumo's Leading Actors-Rikishi and Oyakata

sandanme* rikishi. When one reaches the sandanme, there are changes other than the different level on the banzuke; sandanme rikishi use setta (leather-soled sandals) rather than geta (the wooden clogs) always used by rikishi in the jonidan and below, and men at this level can also wear haori. The next highest level is makushita. Since it is in the second highest level, the formal name for the division is makushita nidanme. Makushita rikishi are allowed to have overcoats,

and instead of the silk crepes used by lower division rikishi to tie their kimono, they can use hakata obi. If rikishi do well in the makushita, they can be promoted to the jumaime, in other words the juryo.

Although the jumaime is on the same second level on the banzuke as the makushita, the names of the rikishi in the division are written in thicker characters. Further, rikishi in the jumaime and above are called sekitori, and compete on all 15 days of tournaments. There are also significant differences in the treatment of rikishi in the jumaime compared with the makushita and lower divisions. As you will have seen on television, rikishi get up on the dohyo after they are called, clap their hands, open both hands wide, do shiko, then take chikaramizu. This water is sometimes called "kiyome no mizu," or "keshomizu," in other words the water is intended to purify oneself. Rikishi are given chikaramizu after they reach the jumaime. "Chikaramizu o tsukeru." is when water is given to rikishi who are taking part in the coming bout. A rikishi on the higashi side is given chikaramizu by the winner of the previous bout, if he was also higashi. If the previous rikishi on the higashi side lost, chikaramizu is given by the rikishi on the same side who will

Chapter 2: Sumo's Leading Actors-Rikishi and Oyakata

be competing in the following bout. In the final bout of the day, if there was no winner on the same side in the previous bout, the rikishi's tsukebito will offer him water.

After the rikishi have been given chikaramizu, they throw salt on the dohyo. Each rikishi has his own way of throwing salt, sometimes exciting the audience. The salt is used for purification. The sacred dohyo is cleansed of evil spirits, and at the same time the rikishi purify themselves and pray for safety. The salt also serves to sterilize cuts and scratches incurred during bouts, however, basically throwing salt is only done from the jumaime upwards.

Also, when rikishi are promoted to the jumaime, they are allowed to have their own haori, hakama (men's formal divided skirts), silk shimekomi*, and a keshomawashi for the dohyoiri. They are also allowed to have their hair arranged in oichomage and have lower rikishi assigned to them as tsukebito. Tsukebito assist sekitori in putting on and taking off their mawashi, and help them wash and take baths. Tsukebito, who are ranked in the makushita and below are also called wakaimon. Rikishi who reach the jumaime have themselves served as tsukebito until this point, and instead having tsukebito assigned to them gives them a very good feeling. Rikishi who reach the jumaime are not assigned just one tsukebito, but two or three. In the makuuchi, above the jumaime, rikishi have three or four attendants, while yokozuna have between eight and ten tsukebito. However, in many cases, heya simply do not have enough wakaimon to serve their own sekitori, in which case lower division rikishi are borrowed from other heya. Being a tsukebito gives wakaimon a chance to study many aspects of the sumo world.

Rikishi who are promoted to the jumaime have akeni. These trunks are made from bamboo, and hold the equipment used by sekitori. Washi (Japanese paper) is wrapped around the bamboo frame, and hardened with shibu (the juice of unripe persimmons) and urushi (lacquer). The riki-

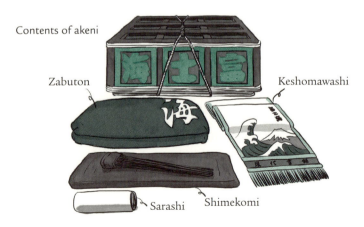

Contents of akeni

Zabuton

Keshomawashi

Sarashi Shimekomi

Chapter 2: Sumo's Leading Actors-Rikishi and Oyakata

shi's name is inscribed in large characters on the akeni. Akeni are about 45 centimeters high, 80 centimeters wide, and 30 centimeters deep, and are heavy at about 10 kilograms when they are filled. They contain the rikishi's shimekomi, keshomawashi, sarashi, and a zabuton for sitting in shitakubeya* and below the dohyo. On the day before basho open, transportation companies collect akeni from all the heya and take them into shitakubeya, where they are kept until the senshuraku, or the 15th and final day of the tournament. In the old days, young rikishi used to carry the akeni themselves. Yokozuna use three akeni.

Another significant change for rikishi who reach the jumaime is that they receive a monthly salary from the Nihon Sumo Kyokai. The salary is substantial and increases the higher they go.

After they reach jumaime, rikishi are addressed as "sekitori" or xxzeki. Rikishi who reach this level are considered to be full-fledged. All rikishi aim to at least reach this level.

Jumaime men who achieve kachikoshi*, or in other words win eight or more bouts, are promoted on the banzuke. If they keep winning at higher ranks, they are promoted to the maegashira ranks in the makuuchi. The maegashira in the makuuchi, ranked below komusubi and above, are known as hiramaku. Hiramaku rikishi who fare well are promoted to the sanyaku, which consists of the komusubi, sekiwake, and ozeki ranks. Komusubi who achieve kachikoshi may be, depending upon the situation with the other ranks, promoted to sekiwake. Sekiwake, on the other hand, do not achieve promotion to ozeki just by achieving kachikoshi. However, komusubi can be demoted to the maegashira ranks with a makekoshi*, or losing record. Rikishi in the upper hiramaku ranks, as well as komusubi and sekiwake, always have to face the yokozuna and ozeki, and it is very difficult for them to achieve kachikoshi. To achieve promotion to ozeki, a rikishi must achieve strong records in three consecutive tournaments at sekiwake. They cannot merely eke out 8-7 records; they must win a total of at least 33 bouts in three tournaments. They must average at least 10 wins per tournament, and unless they win a tournament or defeat the yokozuna and ozeki, they will probably not be able to make a strong impression.

Rikishi who are promoted to ozeki receive a substantial boost in their salary. Yokozuna and ozeki travel by green car (first class) when they use the Shinkansen (bullet train) for

Chapter 2: Sumo's Leading Actors-Rikishi and Oyakata

jungyo. Ozeki are not demoted if they have makekoshi in one tournament. This is very different for all ranks up to sekiwake. Ozeki who have losing records become kadoban* in the following tournament, while retaining their status as ozeki. If they achieve a winning record as kadoban ozeki, they retain their rank. However, ozeki who have makekoshi in kadoban status, in other words, two consecutive losing records, are demoted to sekiwake. However, there is still hope for them, because they are immediately promoted back to ozeki if they win 10 or more bouts in their first tournament down at sekiwake. On the other hand, even if they win 9 bouts in their first tournament back at sekiwake, then cannot achieve promotion back to ozeki with 10 wins in the following tournament. Instead they must start all over again, and achieve strong records in three consecutive tournaments at sekiwake. There have been rikishi who have continued competing even after they have demoted down to the hiramaku and jumaime level. There have also been those who have been demoted from ozeki to the hiramaku level, then returned to ozeki.

After ozeki comes yokozuna, the highest rank in sumo. Very few rikishi go that far. Ozeki must win the championship in two consecutive tournaments or come in as a very close runner-up. Further, they must also have superior quality of character and ample strength. In short, they must have stability, overwhelming strength, as well a strong sense of dignity. Once a rikishi reaches yokozuna, he can never be demoted, even if he has losing records. However, the latter is considered unacceptable. Makekoshi, or a losing record, indicates a lack of strength, and a yokozuna in such circumstances would be expected to take the responsibility inherent in his rank. In other words, there would be no road open to him except retirement.

Shikona
——A Rikishi's Ring Name, Real Names are Acceptable

Shikona are the names of rikishi. Today, the word used for the names of rikishi is shikona, derived from the first two characters of shiko, which rikishi do on the dohyo. However, the original word used different kanji, and the first character appears to have been the name given to people who conducted shinto rituals to drive out evil spirits by stamping on the ground. The word may also refer to humility. Shikona have been used for rikishi since the Edo Era

Chapter 2: Sumo's Leading Actors-Rikishi and Oyakata

(1603-1868).

Traditionally, names of yama (mountains), kawa (rivers), and umi (seas) in the rikishi's home region, as well as parts of the rikishi's master's shikona have often been used for names. However, recently the use of yama, kawa, and umi have been declining. Rikishi are allowed to elect to use their surname as their shikona, for example, Endo. Some shikona are derived from the names of schools or companies which run koenkai (supporters' associations). Further, rikishi can change their shikona later in their career, such as Ama becoming Harumafuji.

With the increase in foreign rikishi, some use phonetic variants of their real name. Some shikona have ambiguous pronunciations, in which cases it is best not to ask the rikishi himself, but rather someone from his heya.

Shikona are usually decided by shisho*, however, rikishi can also decide on their names. The latter may help the shisho, as it saves him trouble.

There are also shussemei, or names that are traditionally used in a heya, and are given to deshi (disciples) once they reach a certain level. These shikona are passed down from generation to generation. Examples are Sakahoko in Izutsu

Beya, Asashio and Takamiyama in Takasago Beya, Dewanohana in Dewanoumi Beya, Kashiwado in Isenoumi Beya, Kotozakura in Sadogatake Beya, and Wakanohana in Futagoyama Beya.

Mawashi——A Rikishi Loses if his Mawashi Comes Off

The fine-looking loincloths which are wrapped around the waist of rikishi are called mawashi. The kanji character, usually pronounced mitsu*, which was originally used for mawashi is also used for fundoshi* (loincloths). The various parts of a mawashi have different names; the

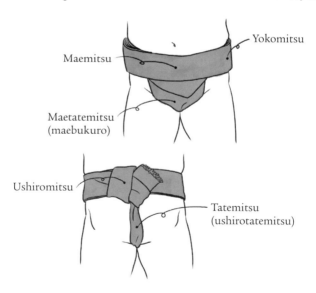

Chapter 2: Sumo's Leading Actors-Rikishi and Oyakata

part which is wrapped around the belly is called maemitsu, the area which covers the vital parts below is called maetatemitsu, the part tied at the front is referred to as yokomitsu, the area at the back is ushiromitsu, while the part below the knot at the back which covers the cleft of the buttocks is called tatemitsu (or ushirotatemitsu). The maetatemitsu is usually just called maebukuro. Rikishi are not allowed to grab an opponent's maetatemitsu or place their fingers in this area, and will lose by hansoku (foul), if they do so. Rikishi are also not allowed to grab the tatemitsu of an opponent. However, if they do so, they will be warned by the gyoji, but a hansoku will not result. Sometimes, this area is grabbed during a bout and part of the buttocks is visible.

The mawashi used by rikishi in the jumaime and above when they are on the dohyo are called shimekomi, while they wear keiko mawashi* for training. Keiko mawashi are white and are made from hardened unsai cotton, the same material used for the soles of tabi. While sekitori use keiko mawashi as-is, in other words, in the original white, rikishi in the makushita and below have theirs dyed black or deep blue, and use the same mawashi both for keiko and for official tournaments.

Shimekomi are made from Hakata woven satin, and are dyed in a variety of colors. They are quite large, at about 9 meters long and 80 centimeters wide. Rikishi fold the wide part of the shimekomi in six to use it. Since it is as large as it is, putting it on is quite a task. It is not easy to put on and take off, as is the yobidashi's tattsukebakama. The mawashi is tied very tightly, but since rikishi are human beings...if they need to urinate, this can be done by slightly moving the maebukuro, but that kind of thing cannot be done for defecation. Therefore, rikishi must endure until their match is over. There are times when they have stomachaches. I won't mention names, but there was once a leakage during a match, and the rikishi involved apologized, saying "Sumi-

Chapter 2: Sumo's Leading Actors-Rikishi and Oyakata

masen." If I recall, I think he lost the bout, and I think he was not able to show much power.

It is fundamental that the mawashi should be worn tightly. If it comes loose and the rikishi's vital parts are exposed, he loses the bout. Therefore, if the mawashi of one or both rikishi becomes loose during a match, the gyoji will halt the bout and tighten the mawashi. Some rikishi have their mawashi tied very tightly, while others have it a little loose. This is part of their strategy. If one's opponent does oshizumo (pushing), having the mawashi tied loosely may dissuade the opponent from pushing by making it look enticing to grasp the mawashi. Conversely, oshizumo rikishi may have their mawashi tied tightly, making it difficult for the opponent to grasp. This also makes it easy to shake off an opponent who does try to get a grip.

The narrow rope-like things hanging from the front of the mawashi are called sagari. They are inserted in the mawashi and hang downwards from it. They are meant to symbolically cover one's private parts, and are made from the warp of the same woven fabric material as the mawashi itself. This material is bundled, frayed by passing through a large comb, hardened into a cylindrical shape by funori (glue), and then dried. The tips are flattened. They are made by the young rikishi in the heya. Glue is placed on each spike in the sagari by hand, and if this is not done well, the sagari are soft. In such cases, the young rikishi may not have known the proper way to prepare the sagari. For good luck, the number of spikes in the sagari is an odd number, such as 17, 19, or 21.

Since sagari are simply tucked in the mawashi, they easily come off during bouts. If rikishi pick up their own fallen sagari, they lose the bout. In reality, rikishi simply do not have the liberty to even think of doing so while they are battling with an opponent. Gyoji immediately pick up sagari which have fallen on the dohyo or have become loose; they must have a keen sense to do this properly.

Nothing is worn under the mawashi, which is never washed. It can only be dried, but not under the sun. Actually it is dirty. It is even said that keiko mawashi should not be washed, but they are actually cleaned, as they become dirty and smelly.

Aside from mawashi, there are also keshomawashi. They are used by rikishi in the jumaime and above for the dohyoiri, as well as by rikishi who perform the yumitorishiki, and are made from silk damask and use silk woven in Hakata and Nishijin (Kyoto). The back of the apron-like part has gold brocade, and the front uses gold and silver thread and other materials for the patterns which are drawn on it. It is fun to look at these patterns or designs on the keshomawashi, which vary from rikishi to rikishi, during the dohyoiri. Only yokozuna and ozeki are allowed to have violet or dark purple colors on the bottom part of the keshomawashi, which is known as the baren. Since keshomawashi use such fine materials and need to be individually handmade, they are very expensive. Rikishi do not have their own keshomawashi made, rather the koenkai and other supporters have them produced to commemorate a promotion or another similar occasion. Therefore, many keshomawshi have the name of the company running the koenkai written on them, while rikishi who are college graduates often have the school badge of their university as the design.

A set of three keshomawashi is needed for the yokozuna dohyoiri. One each is needed for the tachimochi* and tsuyuharai*, and one for the yokozuna himself. This set of three is referred to as a "mitsuzoroi."

A Day in the Life of a Rikishi
―― Keiko Is Done Only in the Morning

Rikishi follow a more-or-less set routine on days when there is no hombasho or jungyo. There are differences in time between heya, but rikishi usually wake up around 6:00 a.m., and immediately begin keiko.

Lower ranked rikishi normally begin keiko first. They start with shiko, then go to the teppobashira (pillar used for teppo) and do teppo moving both their arms and legs. They then spread their knees out, move their feet to the left and right, lower their backs, then stretch their legs with the upper part of their body on the ground. Without taking their feet away, they move forward while sweeping their feet (suri-ashi). Once these preliminary exercises are done, the rikishi do sanban geiko (a series of practice bouts with the same opponent). This is not just three practice bouts, but a number of continuous bouts with the same opponent. This is followed by moshiai, which is done in an elimination format. The winner designates his opponent, and continues doing so until he loses. Losing thus reduces the amount of keiko one does. Designating one's opponent is called "kau," and being selected is termed "ureru."

This is followed by butsukari geiko, in which one rikishi charges and the other absorbs his push forward. This is a defensive form of keiko, and is important to avoid injuries in a defensive position and to strengthen one's legs. The rikishi who is charging pushes into the right chest of the man he is practicing with. At the same time, thrusting is done by pushing with both hands. The rikishi who absorbs the charge gradually falls back to the edge of the dohyo, and tries to hold out there, and knocks his opponent down from his left shoulder. The rikishi who is thrusted down falls fully. This is repeated any number of times. Perhaps the right chest is thrusted against as the heart is on the left side. Once this is over, the rikishi do shiko, matawari, or suriashi, in a crouching position, and then wind up. The keikoba is then cleansed by rikishi in the makushita and below. After sweeping the dohyo, a gohei* (staff with plaited paper streamers) is placed in the middle of the dohyo, and salt is thrown.

This is the typical keiko regimen for an average day, however, on some days rikishi do degeiko (go to other heya to do keiko), or take part in rengo geiko (combined keiko where all the heya in an ichimon*, or group of heya, participate). Rikishi in heya with no sekitori or with only a small number of members often go out for degeiko, as they would not get sufficient keiko in their own heya. Sekitori also go to other heya to practice with potentially difficult opponents.

Keiko sessions last for three or four hours. Once practice is finished, the rikishi bathe and then have chanko for lunch. There is an order in which everyone eats–any guests and the oyakata come first, then the highest ranking rikishi. The shindeshi finally have their chance to eat an hour later, after everyone else is finished. The rikishi then have a nap, and after they wake up, they are free until the evening. Chanko is again served for dinner in the evening, but the volume is slightly less than at lunch. The rikishi are then again free until they go to sleep. Some rikishi stay in the heya and watch television or play games, while others may go out drinking.

In any case, keiko in the heya lasts only a few hours in the morning. Some rikishi elect to go to a gym to train during their free time, and since developing a powerful physique is a necessity, eating and sleep can also be termed part of their work. Actually, rikishi have quite a lot of free time. When I belonged to Isegahama Beya, there was no keiko on Sundays, and the day was a full holiday.

Chapter 2: Sumo's Leading Actors-Rikishi and Oyakata

Chanko——If There is Not Enough Chankosen

Chanko is eaten twice a day. Chanko refers not only to chankonabe, but to all food prepared by rikishi. Thus yakisoba (fried noodles), ramen (soup-noodles), and sashimi (sliced raw fish) can all be termed chanko. However, the strong image attached to the word chanko is from chankonabe. Chankonabe is said to have started during the days when Yokozuna Hitachiyama was active in the Meiji Era (1868-1912), and was intended to facilitate a meal everyone could eat, with cheap, nutritious ingredients.

Chankonabe contains meat, vegetables, fish, and other in-

All food prepared by rikishi is called chanko.

gredients. Rikishi receive an ample amount of nutrition just by two chanko meals in the heya every day. Each heya has its own distinctive flavors and specialities. Sometimes the taste is determined by the okamisan, and sometimes by tradition handed down over generations. The favor also varies according to the chankocho, or the rikishi who supervises its preparation.

A chankocho is a rikishi, in the makushita or below, who supervises the young rikishi in all areas of the preparation of chanko, from the purchase of the ingredients to preparation. Heya with a large number of sekitori are especially likely to have chankocho. All heya have chankoban, or chanko preparation duty for rikishi in the lower divisions. This duty is rotated so as not to deprive rikishi of keiko. Sometimes chankoban is assigned by the heya's wakaimonogashira.

The person in charge of chanko preparation will be entrusted with chankosen (the funds needed to purchase the ingredients), and purchases within this budget, but sometimes this falls short. In such cases, the chankoban needs to decide what everyone will eat that day. This actually happens in each heya fairly frequently. In the heya to which I

Chapter 2: Sumo's Leading Actors-Rikishi and Oyakata

belonged, we had planned to have beef fried in butter, but since there was not enough chankosen, we had to use ham and margarine instead of beef and butter. Grated daikon was added to this. The meal was actually quite delicious. Substitutes like this sometimes become popular dishes. When I belonged to Asahiyama Beya, I was surprised to find fish-paste cake used in place of the meat in sukiyaki. I have also heard a story, though I cannot attest to its veracity, that in Hanakago Beya, water was simply boiled, and everyone was given either one or two eggs and told to eat them in any way they fancied.

Each heya's distinctive tastes in its chanko are handed down through chankoban. Frankly, the chanko in some heya is not very good.

Also, there is an expression in the sumo world that the taste of the chanko soaks in. This means that one accrues experience after entering sumo and becomes rikishi-like both mentally and physically. There are those who leave because they are unable to do this. Sumo is severe, but many rikishi leave because they cannot get used to the customs of the sumo world. There are cases where rikishi simply quit when they are in the vicinity of their hometown on jungyo.

Dohyoiri——The Sekitori Show Their Faces

In the dohyoiri, the rikishi line up in front of the audience in their keshomawashi, to show their faces. There are separate dohyoiri for the jumaime, makuuchi, and yokozuna.

The jumaime dohyoiri takes place when there are still five bouts remaining in the makushita. The makuuchi dohyoiri is staged between the end of the jumaime bouts and the beginning of the makuuchi bouts, or nakairi, and includes all the rikishi from the maegashira up to the ozeki. On odd numbered days, the dohyoiri starts with the rikishi on the higashi side, while on even numbered days, the nishi side rikishi start first. The sharp sound of the yobidashi's clappers is used as a sign to start, with the gyoji first entering the dohyo, followed by the rikishi, in the order of the lowest coming first. The rikishi line up from the left along the outside of the dohyo, with all facing the spectators. The last rikishi, usually an ozeki in the case of the makuuchi, makes a shiii... sound when he has mounted the dohyo, which is known as keihitsu, or heralding. At that moment, all the rikishi turn towards the interior of the dohyo, with their rears facing the audience. They then simultaneously make

Chapter 2: Sumo's Leading Actors-Rikishi and Oyakata

the same movements; they first clap their hands, raise their right hand, then use both hands to grab their keshomawashi and lift it slightly, then raise both arms. This is actually an abbreviated version of the chirichozu, as well as the jodan no kamae, chudan no kamae, and gedan no kamae of the sandangamae, and the shiko, which I will explain later. These movements are executed quickly, and the rikishi then leave the dohyo in order of ranking. During this ceremony, the gyoji crouches in the center, and swings his gunbai.

The makuuchi dohyoiri is followed by the yokozuna dohyoiri. In the yokozuna dohyoiri, all the holders of the rank do not appear together, rather each performs his own dohyoiri separately without any simplification. This is performed as a sumo ritual, but also serves as a shinto ceremony to pray for peace and a good harvest.

In the yokozuna dohyoiri, the participants enter the hanamichi in the order of the yobidashi, gyoji, tsuyuharai, yokozuna, and tachimochi, and then step up on the dohyo with the gyoji leading the way, followed by the tsuyuharai, yokozuna, and tachimochi, who step up together. The tsuyuharai walks in front of the yokozuna, and is supposed to clear the way for the yokozuna. The tachimochi holds a sword from its bottom part, directly horizontal to his right elbow. The tsuyuharai and tachimochi are makuuchi rikishi from the same heya or same ichimon as the yokozuna. The higher-ranked rikishi serves as the tachimochi.

After the three rikishi step up on the dohyo, the yokozuna crouches on the inside of the shobu dohyo, with his tsuyuharai crouching on the left and his tachimochi on the right. The yokozuna spreads both his arms to the left and right. This is called chirichozu, and symbolizes that he is upright and cleanhanded. Thereafter, the yokozuna alone moves to the center of the dohyo, where, facing the shomen, or front side, he claps his hands and does shiko. At this mo-

Tachimochi　　　Chirichozu　　　Tsuyuharai

Chapter 2: Sumo's Leading Actors-Rikishi and Oyakata

ment, the audience shouts "Yoisho." The yokozuna then does the seriagari (rising up part). He lowers his back to go from gedan no kamae to chudan no kamae, and then jodan no kamae, shuffling his feet slowly inward with each move, as he raises his upper body. He then does shiko again twice, goes back to the nijiguchi (p. 111), and does chirichozu again.

When the yokozuna stamps his feet in shiko during the dohyoiri, the gyoji, who is crouching behind him, twirls the tassel of his gunbai in unison with the yokozuna. I have been asked what this represents, and replied that, "Long ago a yokozuna broke wind when he did shiko, and the gyoji thought the smell was very bad, and that's how it originated." Well, it was a joke, but some things in sumo have no real meaning, and there are many movements for which the meaning is obscure. In many cases dignified explanations were simply added later. Well, I think it is ok just to say, "Things used to be done that way, or someone used to do it that way."

After the dohyoiri finishes, the tsuyuharai, yokozuna, and tachimochi leave the dohyo, followed by the gyoji.

The two styles of yokozuna dohyoiri are called the Unryu-gata and the Shiranui-gata. In the seriagari of the Unryu-gata, the yokozuna places his left hand on his side, while inserting his right hand in a somewhat diagonal way. This is said to show both an offensive and defensive stance. In the Shiranui-gata, the yokozuna stetches out both arms during the seriagari. This is said to be an assertively offensive style. Another difference in the two styles of dohyoiri is seen in

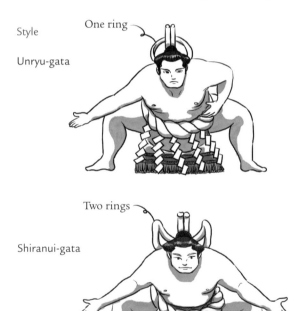

Style

Unryu-gata

Shiranui-gata

the rings on the back of the tsuna (hawser). Unryu-gata yokozuna have one ring, while the Shiranui-gata have two.

The Unryu-gata is based on the style of the dohyoiri of the 20th yokozuna, Umegatani II, however, the dohyoiri of Unryu, the 10th yokozuna, was said to be especially fine, so it was given the name of the latter. The Shiranui-gata takes the name of Shiranui, the 11th yokozuna, who also had an outstanding dohyoiri. However, the Shiranui-gata is actually based on the dohyoiri style of Tachiyama, the 22nd yokozuna. One wonders what Umegatani II and Tachiyama, whose names were not retained for their dohyoiri, are thinking of this in the great beyond.

Bouts——From Entering Shitakubeya to Leaving

The place where rikishi are seen most often is competing on the dohyo. In other words, bouts, for which there is a set of movements starting from before the rikishi enters the dohyo to when he steps down after the bout. Rikishi leave shitakubeya two bouts before their own match. They then walk along the hanamichi until just before they reach the dohyo, at which time they bow. They then sit below the dohyo to await their bout. Rikishi on the east side come down the higashi hanamichi, while those on the west side follow the nishi hanamichi. Hanamichi, or "flower path," sounds like a stylish name. Apparently it dates back to sumai no sechi during the Heian Era (794-1192), when rikishi performed sumo before the emperor inside the Imperial Palace. The rikishi had their hair arranged with an artificial flower, and this is apparently how the word hanamichi originated. Rikishi have their own individual ways of walking down the hanamichi; some walk in a calm way, while others half run down the path. Watching these styles is interesting.

When rikishi approach their seat to await their bout, they bundle their sagari (p. 95) and put a hand out when they pass a judge or the rikishi waiting ahead of them. This is the equivalent of saying something like "Excuse me."

Once they sit down, some rikishi may think of what they will do at the tachiai, however, they are actually expected to closely watch the bouts before their own. The reason for this is that they have the right to call a monoii (dispute the gyoji's verdict), and if they are not watching, they cannot do so.

When the rikishi's bout comes up, the yobidashi calls him up to the dohyo. He then rises and mounts the dohyo

Chapter 2: Sumo's Leading Actors-Rikishi and Oyakata

by climbing the steps up to the ring. The place he steps up to near the tokudawara (on the inner side of the dohyo) is called the nijiguchi, and this is where he bows as he faces his opponent. Rikishi on the higashi side then do shiko facing out of the dohyo under the akabusa, and shirobusa for nishi side rikishi. The rikishi then crouch to be given water. The winner of the previous bout offers him a water ladle. If the higashi side rikishi won in the previous bout, the loser on the nishi side will already have left, so the waiting rikishi on that side will offer him a water ladle. Further, the rikishi who offers water also gives the rikishi on the dohyo a piece of paper cut in two to use as cleaning tissue. This is called chikaragami*. The rikishi who receives it then wipes his mouth and cleans away sweat with it. During this time, the gyoji will have called out the names of both rikishi, saying, "Kataya xxyama," "Konata xxyama," or the like.

The rikishi then take salt from a basket, face in the shomen direction, and throw it. Some rikishi excite the spectators by throwing a large amount of salt, while others throw only a small amount of salt. Once the salt is thrown, the rikishi go to the inner nijiguchi, at which time they may slap their mawashi. Some rikishi drop some salt, or taste it.

Facing his opponent at the nijiguchi, the rikishi crouches, puts both hands down briefly, then rubs his hands together, and claps once. He then moves the palms of his hands upward, opens both arms on the left and right, and puts his palms back down. This ceremonious clapping and rubbing of palms is called chirichozu o kiru, or chiri o kiru (brushing dust off).

After they brush dust off, the rikishi throw salt again, do shiko facing each other, and then go into a crouching position. At this moment, the rikishi gaze at each other eye-to-eye. Sometimes they stare at each other for a while. They then do the shikiri. Facing each other, they touch both hands on the dohyo at the shikiri line, and try to prepare for the tachiai by synchronizing their movements with those of their opponent. They are not allowed to place their hands beyond the shikiri line on their own side. Rikishi who favor migi-yotsu put their left hand down first, while rikishi who do hidari-yotsu put their right hand down. Men who specialize in oshizumo, or pushing, tend to put both hands down simultaneously. In yotsu, both rikishi come to grips with their bodies close to each other, with the men having their right arms above and left arms below in hidari-yotsu, and the reverse in mi-gi-yotsu. For uwate*, one must have his arms above those of his opponent when they are gripping each other, while shitate* is the opposite. Some people call this kenka yotsu, or un-

matching grips, but it means that one rikishi specializes in migi-yotsu, while the other is proficient in hidari-yotsu.

Until the time limit is up, the rikishi continue throwing salt and going through the shikiri. During this time, the yobidashi carry the kensho banners around the dohyo, if there are any prizes to award, and diligently sweep the dohyo, taking care not to get in the way of the rikishi.

The time limit is officially called the shikiri seigen jikan, or in other words, the time limit for shikiri. This is four minutes for the makuuchi, three minutes for the jumaime, and two minutes or less for the makushita and below. This is measured from the moment the yobidashi finishes calling both rikishi to the moment the judge indicates that it is time.

If the rikishi are ready, they can face off in the bout at any point before the time limit. Further, once the time limit has been declared, if rikishi inadvertently take salt or otherwise go out of the dohyo, they automatically lose. Sometimes rikishi are still not ready when the time limit is declared and thus have a false start. Rikishi are supposed to synchronize their movements and be ready to start the bout once the time limit is declared. At one time there were fines for rikishi who had matta, or false starts, but this is no longer the case. However, matta are not considered to be good. Also, the gyoji or head judge can declare a false start. This is called when rikishi do not touch their hands on the dohyo at the tachiai, or when they are not at the shikiri line, or when the tachiai is not done properly. These instances are called "gyoji matta."

I think the most essential point in sumo is the tachiai. The tachiai is very difficult. I think that the outcome of most bouts is decided by how the tachiai is done. The strategy of both rikishi at the tachiai, and the silent tension, is really appealing. This is an area where the weight factor may

Chapter 2: Sumo's Leading Actors-Rikishi and Oyakata

not apply, even though the odds of achieving this may be small, the smaller rikishi may have a chance to win. Therefore, I think one should look closely at the tachiai when watching bouts.

We get to the bout itself, and where winning or losing is decided. Once the bout is over, even if the rikishi have toppled out of the dohyo, they get back on the dohyo, and both men return to their repective higashi or nishi corners, where they bow. The losing rikishi leaves the dohyo, but bows once more before he leaves. The winner goes to the spot where the dohyo protrudes, crouches there and receives the gyoji's kachinanori, or declaration that he is the winner of the bout. At that moment, the winner moves his right hand to the lower right direction. If there is a kensho, he makes a ceremonial hand movement, or tegatana o kiru, with his right hand and picks up the prize from the gyoji, after which he steps down from the dohyo. In the ceremonial hand movement done by the rikishi before he claims the kensho, the rikishi fully stretches out all five of his fingers, then moves his hand to the left, to the right, and finally the middle. This is to show his gratitude to the three guardian deities of bountiful harvests, with the left symbolizing Kamimusubinokami, the right Takamimusubinokami, and the middle Amanominakanushinokami.

The winning rikishi then steps down from the dohyo, and if there is an ensuing bout, he offers water to the next rikishi on his side, then heads back to shitakubeya.

The above is the standard sequence which all bouts follow.

Torikumi are Decided Upon Every Day

By the way, how are the bouts, which change every day, decided upon?

The torikumi hensei kaigi, or bout composition conference is in charge of the matchings, and the head judge, deputy head judge, and rank-and-file judges decide upon the pairings. Gyoji attend and serve as managers and clerks, but they have no right to speak. Their function is to record the pairings decided upon by the judges.

As to when the bouts are decided upon, the pairings for the first and second days are decided two days before the first day, while the matches for the third day onwards are decided upon the day before. In the case of the makuuchi bouts, the hensei kaigi begins at 11:00 a.m., and the rikishi know their next pairings within the same day. This gives them time to think about a variety of strategies. Further, the bouts for the final day are decided upon after the end of the jumaime bouts on the 14th day. The bouts for the first and second days are decided at 9:00 a.m., however, the meeting actually begins earlier than this.

In principle, rikishi face opponents of the same rank, or just above or below them, and yokozuna do not face the lowest maegashira. The yokozuna and ozeki are matched against the sekiwake, komusubi, and high maegashira, so therefore they must face strong opponents every day. However, if lower ranked rikishi continue winning, and achieve a winning record or are in the yusho (championship) race late in the tournament, they are matched against the yokozuna and ozeki.

There are Currently 82 Winning Techniques

The winning techniques in sumo are called kimarite. In 1935 there were 56 techniques, 68 in 1955, 70 in 1960, and 82 from the November 2000 tournament. Rikishi have changed in terms of physique and speed, which has resulted in the emergence of techniques for which there was no suitable kimarite, thus necessitating the creation of new ones.

The most fundamental kimarite are tsukidashi, oshidashi, yorikiri, and four others. There are 13 throwing techniques, including uwatenage, sukuinage, and kubinage, 18 hooking throws, including uchigake, sotogake, kawazugake, and ketaguri, six falling techniques, including izori and shumokuzori, 19 twisting moves, including tsukiotoshi, tottari, uchimuso, and udehineri, and 19 special techniques, such as hikiotoshi, tsuridashi, okuridashi, and utchari.

There are also some non-techniques. This applies when a rikishi does not win by a technique, but rather his opponent loses by an arbitrary action on his own part. This includes isamiashi, where a competitor inadvertently steps out of the dohyo during a bout. There are five such non-techniques, also including koshikudake, when one's knees give way, and tsukite, when a rikishi's hand touches down on the dohyo.

In addition to winning kimarite, there are a great number of skills that enable a rikishi to use a given technique. Examples of this are harite, when one thrusts at his opponent's face with his palm at the moment of the tachiai, to get into a favorable position. Another skill is thrusting at an opponent's throat with the thumb and other fingers in a Y-shape on an open palm. This facilitates winning by oshidashi. Unusual skills include snapping out with both arms in front of one's opponent's eyes at the moment of the tachiai, in what is known as nekodamashi, grabbing an opponent's leg, jumping out of the way, etc. These are surprise strategies that small rikishi sometimes use on large opponents.

There is also the utchari technique. To do this one, one needs to have strong hips. This is also called nimaigoshi. Recently, it has become rare to see rikishi winning through having strong hips. Utchari involves turning the tables by at the edge of the dohyo. Since the winning rikishi also falls, it can result in injuries. This may make rikishi think twice about using the technique. Utchari makes bouts interesting, since one must watch until the end to see who wins. Myobudani and Wakanami were masters of utchari. Myobudani was also so proficient at lifting his opponents, that he was nicknamed the crane.

The Yumitorishiki
―― A Ceremony Performed on Behalf of the Winner

During official tournaments, we see these techniques repeated until all the day's bouts are completed. A rikishi is

Yumitorishiki

then given a bow by the tate gyoji, and performs a ceremony with a set sequence of movements on the dohyo. This is called the yumitorishiki.

The yumitorishiki is performed on behalf of the winning rikishi, therefore the man performing the ceremony must not touch his hand on the dohyo. If he drops the bow, he must raise it with the top of his foot. If the yumi falls out of the dohyo, the yobidashi picks it up, places it on the dohyo, after which the rikishi raises it with the top of his foot. When the yumitorishiki is finished, the yobidashi hits his clappers to signify uchidashi, or the end of the day's program. As for the rikishi who perform the yumitorishiki, most are in the makushita or below and belong to the same heya as one of the yo-

Chapter 2: Sumo's Leading Actors-Rikishi and Oyakata

kozuna. In case something happens to the yumitori rikishi on jungyo, there is always a second man in reserve who can perform the ceremony.

At the time of the yumitorishiki, the fukutate yobidashi (deputy head yobidashi) crouches on the dohyo. When I did this, the gyoji would come to take the yumi from the yobidashi crouching on the dohyo, and the gyoji would in turn give it to the rikishi performing the yumitorishiki. However, now the yobidashi stands up and hands the yumi to the gyoji. I would hit my clappers, after which I would remain in a crouching position until the yumitorishiki was completed. I would then need to stand, but since crouching is uncomfortable, I would not do so fully. I don't know who started this, but I think it is fine. There are no special rules on this.

Actually, the amount of time one needs to crouch during the yumitorishiki is quite substantial, and there were times when I felt like telling the yumitori rikishi to get it over with quickly.

By the way, since there is a bow, it must seem strange that there is no arrow or string. Actually arrows and string do appear. On the final day, winners of the last three bouts, or yakuzumo, receive these things. The winner of the first of these bouts is given an arrow and the second receives string. Since these bouts normally also have kenshokin* (prize money), the winners receive both the arrow or the string together with the monetary prizes. Please look at this closely at the next opportunity you have. The winner of the final bout on the last day is given a bow, and on behalf of the winner, the yumitori rikishi receives the bow and holds the yumitorishiki. Long ago, the yumitorishiki used to be held only on the final day, but has taken place every day since the January 1952 tournament.

Yusho, the Sansho and Kenshokin
——The Makuuchi Yusho Winner Receives Prize Money of 10 Million Yen

When they become rikishi, men aim to become yokozuna or win the yusho. There are championships for every division from the jonokuchi to the makuuchi, but what everyone aims to do once is to win the makuuchi yusho. Formally, it is called the makuuchi saiko yusho. Of course doing so is difficult, but even rikishi who realize that they cannot reach yokozuna still think they might be able to win the yusho. Usually yokozuna and ozeki win the yusho, but once

Chapter 2: Sumo's Leading Actors-Rikishi and Oyakata

in so many years, even a maegashira, in other words, a hiramaku rikishi, wins the yusho. Examples of this are Kyokutenho winning the yusho at Maegashira 7 and Takatorki doing so at Maegashira 14. Sekiwake and komusubi face the yokozuna and ozeki in the first week, so it is especially difficult for them to have a winning streak from the first days. However, in the lower maegashira ranks, most rikishi face opponents of the same level in the first half of the tournament, and if they are in good form, they can continue winning. And if they build up momentum, they may face the yokozuna and ozeki in the last days, and actually defeat them. If the yokozuna are in poor form, and have two or three loses, these lower rikishi may have a chance.

The winner of the makuuchi yusho is awarded the Tennoshihai (Emperor's Cup), yushoki (yusho flag), and other certificates and trophies. The makuuchi yusho winner is awarded 10

million yen, while the jumaime winner takes 2 million yen. Further, the Mainichi Shimbun presents a yusho portrait. These are the portraits of makuuchi tournament winners which are displayed in the Kokugikan. The portraits were hand-colorized black & white photographs until January 2014, and were called yusho shikisai shashingaku until then. At that time Sato Suzue-san, who had painted the portraits, retired. They were replaced by color photographs, and have since been called yusho shashingaku. The portraits are about the size of five tatami mats (about 8 m²) and weigh 80 kilograms. Of course, they cannot be displayed permanently. They are large and take up space, with a new portrait added for every tournament. Eight portraits each are displayed on the east, west, south, and north sides inside the Kokugikan, for a total of 32. They are taken down in order of their age and returned to the winner. Past winners often give these portraits to members of their koenkai or to the school from which they graduated.

After the presentations, there is normally a yusho parade. The tournament winner sets off from the Kokugikan in an open car, and heads to his heya. The yushoki, or championship flag, is carried by a rikishi from the same heya or ichi-

Chapter 2: Sumo's Leading Actors-Rikishi and Oyakata

mon. The parade also starts off from the site of the tournament when it is held outside Tokyo. In the case of the Kyushu Basho, which is held at the Fukuoka International Center, the parade concludes after just going 500 meters down the street in front of the venue.

There are ceremonies remaining after the awards ceremony on the last day. These are the shusse rikishi teuchishiki, or hand clapping ceremony for apprentice rikishi, and the ceremony to see off the gods. The apprentice rikishi who are being presented to the audience step up on to the dohyo with the judges, and all the new rikishi take turns sipping sacred sake. The yobidashi hands the sake cup to the rikishi, fills it with sacred sake, and once the rikishi have all partaken, hits his wooden clappers, and a sanbonjime, or handclapping patter is done. This concludes the ceremony for the apprentice rikishi. When I was pouring the sacred sake, I would always take care to smile. The rikishi were all tense, so I did this to put them at ease. The rikishi would then toss the gyoji up into the air, in the ceremony to send the gods back to heaven. Finally, the yobidashi would hit his clappers to conclude the ceremony.

In the makuuchi, in addition to the yusho, or championship, rikishi ranked at sekiwake or below can be awarded three prizes; the shukunsho (outstanding performance award), kantosho (fighting spirit prize), and ginosho (technique prize). To be eligible to win one of these prizes, rikishi must achieve kachikoshi with at least eight wins. The shukunsho is awarded for upsets over yokozuna and ozeki, or for a record which impacted the yusho race. Rikishi can be awarded multiple prizes in the same basho, and likewise prizes can be shared among multiple rikishi. Sometimes no rikishi may be awarded a given prize. Each prize is worth 2 million yen, and serves to encourage makuuchi rikishi.

In addition, kenshokin, or monetary prizes are awarded just to makuuchi rikishi. These prizes are offered, through the Sumo Kyokai, by private companies, koenkai of rikishi, etc., with each organization required to offer at least 15 prizes per tournament. They are not required to provide prizes for all bouts on a day, rather they are typically given to bouts involving the top-ranking or popular rikishi. The prize package for every 15 bouts is 930,000 yen, or 62,000 yen per bout. The Sumo Kyokai retains 5,300 yen from each prize to defray insertion fees, such as banners and the public address system, and the winning rikishi is awarded the remaining 56,700 yen. If there are 10 kensho for one bout, for example, the winner takes 567,000 yen, thus rikishi can earn more the harder they try to win. No kensho are awarded for a default win. The envelopes handed to the rikishi actually contain only 30,000 yen each. The rest is retained by the Sumo Kyokai to settle year-end tax bills. The remaining funds are included with the allowances a rikishi is awarded when he retires. If this was not done, they would spend all the money!

Jungyo and Hanazumo

In addition to the six annual official tournaments, or hombasho, the Nihon Sumo Kyokai holds regional jungyo, which are managed by the jungyobu (jungyo division). Jungyo are intended to popularize sumodo, help stimulate local regions, and train youths. The promoter of a jungyo is called the kanjinmoto, and is typically a local government, chamber of commerce, Lion's Club, Rotary Club, or the like. Sometimes jungyo are part of an annual event, and are usually held in gymnasiums and similar facilities. The Haru, or Spring Jungyo includes the Kanto, Tokai, and Kinki regions, the Natsu, or Summer Jungyo centers around the

Tohoku, Hokkaido, and Shinetsu regions, the Aki, or Fall Jungyo goes to the Tokai, Hokuriku, Kansai, Chugoku, and Shikoku areas, while the Fuyu, or Winter Jungyo is held in Kyushu and Okinawa.

In the case of jungyo, we arrive at the site the day before. There are a total of about 270 participants, including oyakata, rikishi, gyoji, yobidashi, and tokoyama. The site opens around 8:00 a.m., at which time the yobidashi perform taiko. This is followed by keiko bouts between rikishi in the makushita and below. Simultaneously, popular rikishi shake hands with fans. In addition to shaking hands, the sekitori also give autographs to fans and pose for photos with them. The keiko of the rikishi in the makushita and below is followed by that of the jumaime and makuuchi competitors. The sekitori then do sumo with kids, followed by an explanation of sumo techniques or culture. Torikumi between the rikishi in the makushita and below starts around 11:00 a.m., with breaks for the shokiri and performance of yaguradaiko. Sometimes there is also a demonstration on the dohyo of the arrangement of a rikishi's oichomage. Shokiri is a humorous demonstration of prohibited moves and unusual techniques by two rikishi, and is

Chapter 2: Sumo's Leading Actors-Rikishi and Oyakata

Shokiri

quite interesting, making people laugh.

Sumo jinku (songs) are also sung. Talking of sumo jinku, I even wrote a song. Sumo jinku have four verses, going seven, seven, seven, and five, followed by the words "dosukoi, dosukoi." Rikishi started singing for entertainment somewhere between the later part of the Edo Era and the beginning of the Meiji Era, and it became an established custom. The entrepreneur who became my patron in Kyushu asked me to write a jinku about Inamori-san (former president Inamori Kazuo) of Kyocera. The song was sung before Inamori-san at the yearend party of an organization headed by him. I also have written songs about former Prime Minister Mori Yoshiro for Hakuho-zeki. These songs typically relate the life story of a person.

To go back to the subject of jungyo, the jumaime dohyoiri and torikumi follow the bouts of the rikishi ranked in the makushita and below. There is then an intermission, after which the makuuchi rikishi and yokozuna, clad in keshomawashi, have their dohyoiri. The makuuchi bouts finally begin not long before 2:00 p.m. After the last bout finishes, the yumitorishiki is performed, in the same way as at official tournaments.

On jungyo, we sometimes had lodgings in private residences. We were picked up and seen off, which was fun, but the downside was that we always had to drink during the welcoming parties. If there were popular rikishi involved, relatives and local people would gather, and it was quite a major event.

The Nihon Sumo Kyokai holds events called hanazumo as occasion calls. This includes intai-zumo and tsuizen-zumo (for memorial rites). The later are held to raise funds

Chapter 2: Sumo's Leading Actors-Rikishi and Oyakata

for welfare and charity. Jungyo are also included in these events. What hanazumo have in common is that winning or losing has no effect on one's rank on the banzuke or pay. Hanazumo, like jungyo, includes shokiri and the tying of a yokozuna's tsuna on the dohyo, and also, though it has no connection to sumo, singing contests with popular entertainers.

Intai-zumo is the sumo performance held for a retiring rikishi, with the organizers being the retiring rikishi himself and his heya's koenkai. Rikishi who are ranked in the jumaime and above are members of the Rikishikai (the organization for sekitori), and rikishi who have been members for 30 or more basho are eligible to hold intai-zumo at the Kokugikan. If eligible, the rikishi himself decides whether or not to have an intai-zumo. All members of the Rikishikai participate free of charge. The ceremony can also commemorate the assumption to a toshiyori myoseki of the retiring rikishi. If the retiring rikishi who is having an intai-zumo has assumed a toshiyori name, the event also serves to commemorate that. Intai-zumo include the dampatsushiki, and anyone is welcome to attend if they purchase a ticket.

The dampatsushiki is the ritual in which a retired rikishi's topknot is cut off. Rikishi who have spent at least one tournament ranked in the jumaime and above are eligible to have their dampatsushiki held on the dohyo at the Kokugikan. The retiring rikishi sits in the center of the dohyo, dressed in a crested hakama. Members of the koenkai, relatives, rikishi, and others take turns to cut his hair. Finally, his master steps up on to the dohyo to complete the ceremony by cutting off his otabusa, or topknot.

Some rikishi have their dampatsushiki in their own heya or another place, rather than the Kokugikan.

Rikishi I Remember——Hokutenyu Had Style

I liked Tochinishiki when I was a child. He was the 44th yokozuna. He had a wide range of techniques, and even though he was not very large, he was strong. He won 10 championships. After entering sumo, I had few personal relationships with rikishi, however, there was one rikishi I admired. He was Hokutenyu, who reached ozeki. He had a very natural style for everything from entering the hanamichi, throwing salt, and even the way he stepped down from the dohyo. He never put on airs, was never tense, and he had really good taste. Further, his sharp uwatenage technique was superb. It can be said that he had a model uwatenage. He was strong in his rivalry with Konishiki, and ended up winning a majority of their bouts. He competed with everyone, including the large Konishiki, seriously, and I admired the way in which he took on all opponents with the same style, in other words with his own way of doing sumo. He even managed to defeat Konishiki in gappuri-yotsu. Konishiki was basically weak at yotsu-zumo. Hokutenyu suffered from diabetes, injured his knee in a bout with Konishiki, and ended up not reaching yokozuna. I had hoped he would be promoted to yokozuna. After retiring, he opened Hatachiyama Beya, but died of illness when he was in still in his 40s.

I socialized with Hakuho-zeki. Before I retired, I introduced him to a person from Kyushu who became a patron of mine. I planted cherry tree seedlings with Hakuho-zeki on his cherry tree hill. Hakuho-zeki is a wonderful person, and he sometimes talks about interesting subjects when he is interviewed after winning tournaments. I think this in one of his wonderful qualities. We even drank together. I have good memories of him.

To Become an Oyakata, One Must Succeed to One of the 105 Toshiyori Myoseki

There is a retirement age for gyoji, tokoyama, and yobidashi. If there are no special problems, one can work until 65. However, this does not apply to rikishi. They follow many career paths after retiring. The first career choice is to become an oyakata, but not all retiring rikishi can do so. Officially called toshiyori, they are usually referred to as oyakata.

One must meet certain conditions to become a toshiyori. The first is that the former rikishi must succeed to a toshiyori myoseki (toshiyori name). This is often referred to as toshiyori kabu (stock) or oyakata kabu, but is not the official term used by the Nihon Sumo Kyokai. They may be called Isegahama Oyakata or Kokonoe Oyakata, but Isegahama and Kokonoe are actually toshiyori myoseki. There are currently 105 toshiyori myoseki, and if they are all occupied, one cannot become a toshiyori.

To succeed to a toshiyori myoseki, retiring rikishi must have Japanese citizenship. To become toshiyori, foreign rikishi must first become naturalized Japanese citizens. Further, to qualify, rikishi must have been ranked in the

Chapter 2: Sumo's Leading Actors-Rikishi and Oyakata

makuuchi for a total of 20 or more tournaments, or have been in the makuuchi and/or jumaime for a total of 30 tournaments and over. Rikishi who have been ranked in the sanyaku for a single tournament are also automatically eligible, as are, of course, former yokozuna and ozeki. Even if they do not have a toshiyori myoseki, former yokozuna are allowed to become toshiyori, under their shikona, for five years, or three years in the case of ozeki.

Further, there are also ichidai toshiyori, or one generation toshiyori. In the past, retiring yokozuna who did not have their own toshiyori name were allowed to become toshiyori for only one generation, using their shikona, as a special privilege. This was called the ichidai toshiyori system, but was abolished. Former yokozuna can now remain for five years without their own toshiyori name, however, the Nihon Sumo Kyokai can also award a special ichidai status to great yokozuna who have exceptional contributions. Taiho, Kitanoumi, and Takanohana were all granted ichidai toshiyori status. Chiyonofuji was also offered this, but declined, and instead succeeded to the Kokonoe toshiyori name.

Rikishi who are not able to acquire toshiyori and thus

do not become oyakata, have a wide range of career choices. Some remain in the sumo world as wakaimonogashira or sewanin, others open chanko restaurants, or engage in a variety of occupations. Of course, the vast majority of retiring rikishi start new careers outside sumo. Yobidashi, like me, can work to the retirement age of 65, but this does not apply to rikishi. Sumo is a severe world.

Oyakata Operating Heya and Oyakata Belonging to Heya

Some people may think that all toshiyori, or in other words oyakata, operate their own heya. This is not the case. There are currently 43 sumo beya. While there are changes in the number of heya, this represents less than half the total number of oyakata.

Sumo beya train rikishi on behalf of the Nihon Sumo Kyokai, and are operated by oyakata (toshiyori). The oyakata who operates a heya is called the shisho, or heya-mochi oyakata. Oyakata who do not operate their own heya are called heya-tsuki oyakata or toshiyori. Rikishi, gyoji, yobidashi, tokoyama, and others are all members of the Nihon Sumo Kyokai, and must belong to a sumo beya. This

Chapter 2: Sumo's Leading Actors-Rikishi and Oyakata

includes heya-tsuki oyakata, most of whom belong to the same heya as when they were in active competition. Most of them help to coach the rikishi in the heya to which they belong, though sometimes they can also be assigned to help out in other heya.

When I joined Isegahama Beya, there was an oyakata called Tateyama, former Sekiwake Hatasegawa. He had been a small rikishi with superb technique, and was nicknamed sumo no kamisama (the god of sumo). He was Isegahama Oyakata's father-in-law, in other words Terukuni's wife's father. When Tateyama Oyakata came over, the atmosphere in the heya would tense up. Isegahama Oyakata was a quiet man, so perhaps Tateyama Oyakata felt that he needed to be strict. He was a good speaker, and even answered questions from lawmakers in the Diet on behalf of the Sumo Kyokai.

A heya can be operated somehow with as few as five deshi. However, this depends upon the degree of support to the oyakata himself, as well as the heya's rikishi available from its koenkai. If a heya has makuuchi and sanyaku rikishi, there are likely to be many supporters, which makes operating it easier. If there are yokozuna or ozeki, things are even easier. Heya are now often buildings. Oyakata play an essential role in the raising of rikishi.

Many heya are handed over to the next generation, and in my case, Kiyokuni took over from my first oyakata, Isegahama. Kiyokuni built a new building, and the deshi moved there. Not many people lived in the old oyakata's heya. The old heya building was originally the oyakata's private property, so naturally rent had to be paid. In such cases, it is better for the succeeding oyakata to have a new building constructed using his own funds.

Few heya have their own premises in cities where official tournaments outside Tokyo are held, so they borrow sites where keikoba can be constructed. Sometimes, the oyakata himself searches for such sites, and the koenkai may help out with introductions, etc. Ryokan are sometimes rented out, and the open lots are rented to build temporary dohyo in prefabricated structures.

Some heya cease to exist. I experienced that. Not only rikishi, but also gyoji, yobidashi, and tokoyama must belong to a heya. In such cases, everyone must move to another heya. Since one does not want to be told they are not needed, it is necessary to always work in a reliable fashion.

Chapter 2: Sumo's Leading Actors-Rikishi and Oyakata

Okamisan Have a Role Akin to that of Mothers

Rikishi refer to the wife of the oyakata of the heya to which they belong as okamisan. This refers not only to the wife of the master, but also to the wives of the other oyakata who are attached to the heya.

Okamisan who are wives of oyakata who operate heya function as de facto mothers of the rikishi, and in addition to helping shindeshi with their personal lives, take care of the heya's finances, the heya's koenkai and visitors who want to watch keiko. The okamisan also handles arrangements for parties as well as relations with other heya. The degree to which they are involved in this varies from okamisan to okamisan. I think women who are very hardworking, me-

Okamisan

thodical, or skilled in socializing are suited for okamisan, and okamisan who show their feelings too readily are not the best. Further, oyakata who are bachelors, of course, have no okamisan. There are actually some heya like that.

Shindeshi often borrow money from okamisan. They initially receive only a small allowance and thus are often short of money. So they ask for okamisan's help. This practice is called hagami (an IOU) o ireru in the sumo world. When the money is returned, the IOU is torn up. I have heard that this is called hagami (the paper is torn up) when the money is returned.

When I entered Isegahama Beya, the okamisan was in her 50s, in other words about my mother's age. She was a good okamisan, and I often expressed my thoughts to her. Once, not long after I entered the heya, the oyakata gave me 30 yen and asked me to call a certain telephone number. I then mentioned to the okamisan that I had been given a number to call. She said, "I understand. That's alright." It seems that the oyakata had a well...mistress. Apparently he wanted to call his mistress to say that the okamisan would be out today. It would have been better if the oyakata had actually explained this to me, but he probably thought there was no

Chapter 2: Sumo's Leading Actors-Rikishi and Oyakata

need to discuss such matters with a shindeshi like me. Perhaps as a result of a quarrel between the two of them, this situation never recurred. The okamisan knew everything. She had been brought up by the old Tateyama Oyakata, and she had actually been a foundling. She told me this. She had experienced hardship but was a warm person.

Managers

Many heya have managers. Most of these are former rikishi who retired in the makushita and lower divisions, and thus have a wide range of expertize about how their heya operates. However, managers do not belong to the Nihon Sumo Kyokai, but rather are employed by the heya to which they belong, and receive their salary from the oyakata. Managers handle the interface with the koenkai, as well as a wide range of duties pertaining to the operation and management of the heya.

Koenkai

——Membership is Available from 10,000 Yen Upwards

Heya have organizations called koenkai, or supporter clubs. These groups provide backup to heya, and many have both individual and corporate memberships. Fees vary from heya to heya, and prerogatives of membership also differ. There are differences according to the fees paid, but some heya invite members to sit in the tamari-seki (ringside seats) or masu-seki (box seats on the first floor), while other heya invite them to have chanko meals after keiko. All heya send the sumo calendar and banzukehyo to their koenkai members. Heya also invite members to events, and provide opportunities to meet with the rikishi. Some heya offer koenkai memberships tailored to women or young people. It is not difficult to become a koenkai member, and annual dues start from about 10,000 yen.

There are also koenkai for individual rikishi, often centering around the hometowns or regions of the rikishi, or the schools they graduated from. The first koenkai was established for Dewanoumi Beya, to which Hitachiyama belonged in 1904. He had just become the 19th yokozuna. This koenkai was called the Hitachiyama Kai.

Of course, while these koenkai are important, the fans who watch sumo on the second floor of the Kokugikan are also important. If sumo is popular, the second floor will be full, but in times of lesser popularity, there are empty seats.

It is therefore very important that ordinary fans purchase tickets for the second floor.

There are Six Ichimon

When I was talking of sumo, I mentioned the Dewa Ichimon. This refers to a group of heya surrounding the head house. This starts with deshi of a master branching out and establishing their own heya. In this way, groups of heya with common routs are linked like families.

Today, there are five ichimon other than Dewanoumi, namely Tokitsukaze, Takasago, Nishonoseki, Isegahama, and Takanohana, for a total of six. All heya belong to an ichimon. At the end of my career, I belonged to Asahiyama Beya, which closed after the January 2015 tournament. Asahiyama Beya belonged to the Isegahama Ichimon.

At the beginning of the Showa Era (1926-1989), a system was established whereby rikishi from different heya in the same ichimon did not compete with each other in official tournaments. This was very advantageous to yokozuna and ozeki who belonged to the same ichimon. This was changed in the January tournament of 1965 to a system whereby only rikishi from the same heya did not compete against each other. This was a much fairer system. In the case of playoffs, rikishi from the same heya do have to compete with each other on the dohyo, as a winner has to be determined.

Further, some rikishi have been brothers or relatives, in which case they do not face each other on the dohyo, even if they are from different heya. I think the rule applies to relatives within the fourth degree of kinship. In the early 1960s, Hasegawa was pitted against his uncle, Shikinohana, when he was in the upper makushita ranks and vying for promotion to the jumaime. The matching was canceled. Not having relatives compete against each other was an unwritten rule until 2009, when it was made into an official rule. However, this does not apply to playoffs for the championship, such as that between Wakanohana and Takanohana.

Chapter 3

Enjoying Sumo

Sumo is Said to Have Originated with Nomi no Sukune

Sumo has such a long history that it is called the kokugi (national sport) of Japan. To go back to its beginnings, the *Kojiki*, which was compiled in the Nara Era (710-794), mentions a contest of strength for the Izumo realm involving Takeminakatanokami and Takemikazuchinokami, while the *Nihon Shoki* describes a mythical bout between Nomi no Sukune and Taima no Kehaya in front of the Emperor. The word sumo first appears in the *Nihon Shoki*, in a description of sumo between maids-in-waiting at the court of Emperor Yuryaku. According to this story, a strong man called Taima

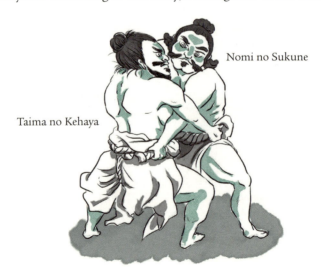

Chapter 3: Enjoying Sumo

no Kehaya boasted that there was nobody stronger than he was. Hearing that, Emperor Suinin inquired as to whether there was anyone of equal strength. He was told by a servant that there was a brave warrior by the name of Nomi no Sukune in the Izumo region. The servant suggested that a bout take place between the two men. Nomi no Sukune was stronger, and broke Taima no Kehaya's rib, then killed him by stamping on his back. Unlike modern sumo, contestants were allowed to strike their opponents, like today's martial arts.

In this way, Nomi no Sukune became the founder of sumo. There is a sumo jinja (shrine) in the precints of the

Nomi no Sukune jinja in Sumida-ku.

Daihyozu jinja in Sakurai-shi in Nara-ken. This is where Nomi no Sukune and Taima no Kehaya clashed.

Further, there are Nomi no Sukune jinja, which enshrine the founder of sumo, in three places. One is in Tatsuno-shi in Hyogo-ken, and is said to be the place where Nomi no sukune died while returning from Izumo.

Another is in Tokyo's Sumida-ku, and was established in 1884, during the Meiji Era (1868-1912). It was built through the efforts of the first Takasago Uragoro, who had his heya in the vicinity, and is situated where the Tsugaru family used to have its residence. When the conference to decide upon bouts meets just before each of the three annual Tokyo Basho, the rijicho of the Nihon Sumo Kyokai, the shimpan bucho (head judge), and others attend the Nomi no Sukune Jinja Reisai (Nomi no Sukune Festival) at the shrine. New yokozuna also perform the dohyoiri there. Within the grounds of the shrine, there is a monument called Rekidai Yokozuna no Hi (Monument to the Yokozuna), with two plaques. One lists the names of all the yokozuna from the first, Akashi Shiganosuke, to the 46th, Asashio Taro. Since this plaque is full up, a second one lists all the yokozuna from the 47th, Kashiwado Tsuyoshi, onwards.

Chapter 3: Enjoying Sumo

Monuments to all yokozuna in history.

In 2013, a Nomi no Sukune Jinja was built within Izumo Taisha. Until then, Nomi no Sukune had been worshiped together with another god.

I mentioned Akashi Shiganosuke, and I would like to elaborate a bit on him. He is said to have been the first yokozuna, but it is not known whether he really existed. There is a banzuke for a kanjin-zumo tournament held in Yotsuya Shio-cho in the first year of the Kanei Era (1624), which lists him as an ozeki from Utsunomiya. However, it is said that the banzuke is fake, and not being a researcher myself, I cannot venture an opinion as to whether or not it is genuine. In 1900, when Jinmaku Kyugoro, the 12th yokozuna, formulated a list of the yokozuna, he declared that Akashi Shiganosuke was the first yokozuna. Akashi's name appears in old records of the Edo Era (1603-1868). For instance, Santo Kyoden, a novelist, wrote a book entitled the *Kinsei Kiseki-Ko*, which mentions that Akashi was given the title of Hinoshita Sumo Kaizan, after defeating the powerful rikishi Niodayu (who was ozeki on the east side, while Akashi was ozeki on the west side), who was invited to Kyoto. This is similar to another word, hinoshita kaizan. The first word, hinoshita, means tenka, or the whole country, while kaizan means the

Chapter 3: Enjoying Sumo

first person to do something. In other words, a rikishi of unequaled strength. This story led Akashi Shiganosuke to be called the first yokozuna.

The forerunner of today's sumo was sumai no sechi, also called sumai no sechie. The meaning of this word is praying for a bumper crop. These ceremonial performances were held for the Imperial Court from the Nara Era to the Heian Era (794-1192), with the strongest rikishi from all over

Sumai no sechi

the country gathering to take part in sumo before the Emperor. There was no dohyo, with the bouts taking place on the open ground. The competitor who forced the hand or elbow of his opponent to the ground first was the winner. Hitting and kicking were prohibited. Prohibited throws were gradually standardized and have been passed down to today's sumo. According to records, the first sumai no sechi was held in the 6th year of the Tempyo Era, or 734, with Emperor Shomu attending. These exhibitions were discontinued during the reign of Emperor Takakura in the 4th year of the Shoan Era, or 1174, when the warriors of the Minamoto and Taira clans came to the forefront, resulting in a time of strife.

Sumo itself continued in the Kamakura Era (1185-1333), in which the government was controlled by warriors. Sumo was held as entertainment at the front, and joran-zumo performances were held for Minamoto no Yoritomo and many years later for Oda Nobunaga. Further, the *Soga Monogatari* (Soga Story), of the Sogakyodai no Adauchi, mentions a sumo bout held between Kawazu Saburo and Matano Goro in 1176 in Amagisan in Izu, with Kawazu winning. Kawazu's kimarite is said to be the origin of the contemporary kawazugake technique, but there appears to be no evidence to support this. Kawazugake involves throwing an opponent by putting one's leg between their legs, then using one's arm on the same side to thrust at the opponent's neck, and then fall back together. The aim is, of course, to get the opponent to touch down first. It is a last ditch throw, and is rarely used. Takanonami used this technique to topple the higher-ranked Akebono and Takanohana.

Takanonami died recently at an early age. He was a gentle person. I think it was about the time he reached the jumaime, and when Wakanohana and Takanohana, who were from the same heya, had overtaken him in gaining promotion to the makuuchi. I asked him during keiko on jungyo whether he had any regrets about having been overtaken. He simply said he would do his best. He ended up reaching ozeki.

From the Edo Era to Today
———There was a Crisis After the Meiji Restoration

During the Edo Era, Joran-zumo were held for Tokugawa Ienari and other shogun, in addition to which the bakufu gave permission for kanjin-zumo (to benefit temples) to be held. However, this permission system was not immediately granted. At the beginning of the Edo Era, there were tsuji-zumo performances in roadside tents, with ronin (masterless samurai) and gangs of rowdies participating, resulting in brawls. Kanjin-zumo was intended to establish or donate to shrines and temples, however, for-profit kanjin-zumo increased, resulting in the bakufu prohibiting both tsuji-zumo and kanjin-zumo. Daimyo sponsored rikishi, but the bakufu placed many restrictions on sumo, such as requiring that mawashi be made of cotton rather than silk, and prohibiting the use of shikona. However, sumo had become firmly established as entertainment for the common people of Edo. Even though it was officially prohibited, kanjin-zumo was held at the Fukagawa Hachimangu and other venues. In 1684, Ikazuchi Gondayu became the kanjinmoto (organizer) and was officially granted approval by the shogunate's section responsible for temples and shrines to hold a tournament at the Tomioka Hachimangu. This led to a permission system for kanjin-zumo, and from then on, sumo became established as a type of amusement for the masses, and nishikie (woodblock prints) of popular rikishi were sold.

The 4th Yokozuna Tanikaze Kajinosuke and the 5th Yo-

Chapter 3: Enjoying Sumo

kozuna Onogawa Kisaburo were among the strongest competitors of the Edo Era. Tanikaze, who was from the Mutsu region (today's Sendai) contributed greatly to sumo's popularity from the Anei to Kansei Eras of the late 18th century. He achieved a record of 63 consecutive wins, which was broken by Onogawa, from the Omi region in today's Shiga-ken. Bouts between these two yokozuna were very popular. They were followed by Raiden Tameemon from the Shinano region in today's Nagano-ken. Raiden, who was famous for his superhuman strength, had a record of 254 wins and only 10 loses. However, for some reason, he was never promoted to yokozuna. As his strength was obviously at the level of a yokozuna, his name is included on the list of yokozuna on the Yokozuna Rikishihi (Yokozuna Rikishi Memorial) at the Tomioka Hachimangu in Tokyo's Koto-ku, under the inscription of murui rikishi Raiden Tameemon (unparalleled rikishi Raiden Tameemon).

After the Meiji Era began, sumo slipped into a very difficult period. This was due to rikishi having been sponsored by daimyo (feudal lords). The daimyo system ended, leaving the rikishi without adequate funds. Another factor was the introduction of Western culture; some thought it was uncivilized that rikishi would compete naked except for their mawashi, and with topknots. There were even calls for the abolition of sumo. However, the rikishi endured even in poverty and the sumo world took a number of steps to modernize. One of these was that women, who had previously only been allowed to watch bouts on the senshuraku, or final day, were admitted on all days of tournaments from 1872, with the exception of the first day. Further, from 1877, women were allowed to watch bouts on all days of tournaments.

Emperor Meiji's imperial visits to sumo resulted in sumo's popularity being restored. His initial visit to sumo was in the 14th year of Meiji Era, or 1881, but it was his fourth visit, at the Hama Detached Palace in Shiba in 1884 which proved especially memorable. In that performance, Umegatani I, the 15th yokozuna, had a great bout with Maegashira 3 Odate, which included two mizuiri and concluded as a hikiwake (draw). Umegatani was already a yokozuna by this time, but he initially declined to participate, as he did not have an appropriate set of keshomawashi for the dohyoiri. The great statesman Ito Hirobumi intervened and provided him with funds for a new set of keshomawashi.

To stabilize sumo's popularity, the first Kokugikan was

Chapter 3: Enjoying Sumo

completed in Ryogoku in 1909. Until then, tournaments were held outdoors with a tent structure. However, this system could only accommodate about 2,000 spectators, but the new Kokugikan could hold 13,000 people. The name Kokugikan appeared to have been first proposed by the then Oguruma Oyakata. There were other naming candidates such as Shobukan or Sumokan. The name Kokugikan proved to be a good choice and has continued until today. There has also been an assumption since then that sumo is Japan's kokugi. The first Kokugikan burnt down in 1917. It was replaced by the second Kokugikan which survived, albeit damaged by fire, both the Great Kanto Earthquake in 1923 and bombing during World War II. After the war, the Kokugikan was moved to Kuramae, then back to Ryogoku in 1985.

Sumo tournaments were organized by a structure called the kaisho from the Edo Era. This became the Tokyo Ozumo Kyokai in the Meiji Era, was renamed the Dai Nihon Sumo Kyokai in the Taisho Era (1912-1926), and is today referred to as the Koeki Zaidan Hojin Nihon Sumo Kyokai.

The two greatest rikishi of this period were Hitachiyama in the Meiji Era and Futabayama, who became the 35th yokozuna in 1937.

The 19th Yokozuna Hitachiyama would allow his opponents to do whatever initial moves they chose to do, and then would slip his hands under his opponent's arms to reach the underside of his mawashi. Hitachiyama would then freeze his opponent's movement and drive him out of the dohyo with a technique called izumigawa. He was a very dignified rikishi and contributed greatly to reforming and improving sumo. Due to his superior personality, he was called "kakusei" or "ontai."

Futabayama never made false starts at the tachiai and was always ready to take on his opponents. He was an exceptional yokozuna, winning 12 championships in 15 tournaments, including five consecutive titles, and had eight yusho with perfect records. He also won 69 consecutive bouts, a record that has never been broken.

Nihon Sumo Kyokai

The Koeki Zaidan Hojin Nihon Sumo Kyokai organizes official tournaments as well as jungyo (regional tours). The organization pays the sekitori, gyoji, yobidashi, tokoyama, and others in sumo, and maintains the traditions of sumo,

Chapter 3: Enjoying Sumo

which is known as the kokugi.

The Nihon Sumo Kyokai is operated by former rikishi who have retired from active competition and have assumed toshiyori myoseki. The organization includes the Sumo Kyoshujo (Sumo School), shido fukyubu, seikatsu shidobu, jigyobu, shimpanbu, chihobashobu, jungyobu, kohobu, and the Sumo Hakubutsukan, etc. The Sumo Hakubutsukan, or Sumo Museum is housed inside Ryogoku Kokugikan, and was launched in 1954, when Kuramae Kokugikan opened. The museum moved to Ryogoku Kokugikan in 1985, and displays materials related to sumo, but there is no permanent exhibition, instead the content is changed every two months. In other words, you never get tired of the museum, no matter how many times you visit it. Normally admission to the museum is free of charge, but it is open only to ticket holders during the Tokyo Basho, and is closed during the new year holidays, and on every weekend and national holidays.

There is also an external advisory organization known as the Yokozuna Shingiiinkai (Yokozuna Deliberation Council). It was established in 1950, and consists of members who are not in the sumo world. The organization makes recommendations on the promotion and retirement of yokozuna.

The banzuke hensei kaigi (banzuke formulation conference) makes recommendations on whether or not rikishi should be promoted to yokozuna, and an unanimous vote in the rijikai results in promotions, however, the Yokozuna Shingiiinkai is first consulted. To make a recommendation for promotion, at least two-thirds of the members of the committee must vote in favor. Rikishi who do not have approval from this committee have been passed over for promotion to yokozuna.

One also frequently sees mention of a "keiko soken" in the news on TV and others. The official name of this event is the Yokozuna Shingiiinkai keiko soken, and it is held by the Nihon Sumo Kyokai before the Tokyo Basho in January, May, and September. It gives viewers the opportunity to see what condition rikishi are in before the tournament. The top rikishi, from the upper makuuchi to yokozuna, participate.

The Yokozuna Shingiiinkai, the members of which receive no remuneration, has only the functions described above.

Chapter 3: Enjoying Sumo

While not part of the Nihon Sumo Kyokai itself, there is an ijiin, or special supporter system. The judges and waiting rikishi sit beside the dohyo, and there are ringside seats immediately behind them. This area is usually referred to as "suna kaburi." Some of these seats are occupied by the ijiin, and only they can use them. Ijiin are individuals or organizations which backup the Nihon Sumo Kyokai's operations, and their fees help support the latter. Koenkai support individual heya and are different from ijiin.

Ijiin are divided among the cities where tournaments are held, with separate members for Tokyo, Osaka, Nagoya, and Fukuoka. This enables members to attend hombasho in their own city, and sit in the seats reserved for them. Eating and drinking, and smoking, all of which are pleasures of watching sumo, are not permitted in the ringside seats reserved for the ijiin. One of the privileges of the ijiin is that they are given a vote in determining the winners of the sansho (three prizes). This does not mean that every member has a vote, rather they select a single member from among them in each city, to vote.

Ijiin memberships are renewed every six years. The fees apply only to three Tokyo Basho, with the cost being high at over 3.9 million yen per year. The fees for the out-of-Tokyo Basho are over 1.3 million yen per tournament.

Seeing Sumo Beya —— Watching Keiko

The enjoyment of watching sumo is not limited just to official tournaments and jungyo. It is also interesting to watch keiko, or training. Other than during official tournaments, rikishi usually do keiko at their own heya. It would be nice to watch the strong keiko of one's favorite rikishi.

It is up to the heya as to whether or not to allow visitors to watch their keiko. This differs from heya to heya. Some heya have large windows which allow people outside to freely observe keiko, while other heya allow fans to reserve in advance and actually sit on cushions inside and watch from there. Basically, it is ok for fans to watch keiko, however, some heya give priority to members of their koenkai. Some heya may only allow members of the koenkai to watch. In principle, visitors must always put their cell phones on silent mode or turn off the power altogether. Some heya permit photography, but flash photos are prohibited. Spectators must not converse with each other.

The websites of some heya may have information on

Chapter 3: Enjoying Sumo

whether visitors can watch keiko. Another possibility is to directly phone the heya and ask. Of course, there is no charge to watch keiko, but some people take presents to heya. Some heya even list presents they would welcome on their websites. This avoids the need to think of what to bring. There are even heya which permit spectators to sample their chanko, or even partake of a chanko meal if they pay to do so.

Watching Sumo at the Kokugikan

It is interesting to watch sumo on television, but going to see the bouts at Ryogoku Kokugikan gives one a perspective that cannot be experienced otherwise. One of these perspectives is the sound of rikishi when they clash on the dohyo. The full impact of this cannot be conveyed on television.

Further, one can only see what the camera focuses on when watching television. Sumo centers around rikishi, and most of them can be seen on TV, however, yobidashi have many types of movements, especially between bouts, which can only be seen by attending tournaments.

The Kokugikan has box seats on the first floor, classed as tamari-seki, masu-seki A, B, and C, as well as Western-

Chapter 3: Enjoying Sumo

style seats also divided into A, B, and C, depending upon the proximity to the dohyo. There are also jiyu-seki, or unreserved seats. All tickets other than jiyu-seki are for reserved seats, so please place your orders quickly. Jiyu-seki tickets are sold at the ticket window on the day itself. One cannot eat, drink, or take photographs from the tamari-seki area. This enables one to totally concentrate on watching the bouts. However, one can eat, drink alcoholic and other beverages, or take photographs from any other seat.

Tickets may be purchased from the website of the Sumo Annaijo. However, the only seats they sell are in boxes on the first floor. On the other hand, if one purchases tickets from them, the entrance is not the usual one, but rather the Sumo Annaijo's own gate, and a kimono-clad attendant known as a dekata will show you to your seat, and also take all your orders for food and drink. The Sumo Annaijo used to be called sumo jaya or simply chaya (tea houses), and I think everyone is more familiar with that term. They have guided spectators since the Edo Era, and have always sold tickets, food and drink, and souvenirs. In 1957, the Sumo Annaijo was reformed. For example, 20 shops, with names such as Takasagoya, were given numbers, from 1 to 20, by

Dekatasan

The contents are...

Rice crackers

Lunch box

Sweet chestnuts

Anmitsu

Yakitori

which they are known today. These shops are operated by the Kokugikan Service Co., Ltd.

Although the most popular rikishi appear on the dohyo in the makuuchi bouts in the late afternoon, sumo begins

Chapter 3: Enjoying Sumo

in the morning. If you have the time, please go and watch sumo from the first bout in the morning. You will discover many things by doing this. The doors open in official tournaments at 8:00 a.m., with the jonokuchi bouts starting at 8:30. Matches of the jonidan, sandanme, and makushita follow. The jumaime dohyoiri takes place at 2:15 p.m., and is followed by the bouts of the same division. The number of people watching is still quite small at that time, and it is possible to view the bouts in a relaxed manner. Once the jumaime is over, the dohyoiri of the makuuchi rikishi and yokozuna takes place from 3:40 p.m. Please see all of this. The makuuchi bouts take place from after 4:00 p.m., and all the bouts are over by 6:00 p.m.

One can wander around the Kokugikan before the jumaime and makuuchi bouts begin. There are many shops where one can purchase souvenirs, and it is possible to have a meal at a restaurant. The Kokugikan is famous for its yakitori. There is a yakitori factory in the basement of the Kokugikan, which produces 50,000 yakitori sticks per basho.

During the time when the makushita bouts are taking place, and one may be browsing around the shops, the makuuchi rikishi enter the Kokugikan. If one stands outside, it is possible to see the sekitori closeup as they enter. When the time comes for the bouts between the sekitori, those who also wish to listen to the bouts on the radio can do so. In addition to NHK's FM broadcasts, the Nihon Sumo Kyokai has its own station, Dosukoi FM, the broadcasts of which start at 3:00 p.m. Although NHK broadcasts can be heard outside the Kokugikan, Dosukoi FM can only be listened to within the Kokugikan. Spectators have the choice of either bringing their own FM-capable radio, or borrowing a radio inside the Kokugikan. The charge for borrowing a radio is 2,100 yen, but 2,000 yen of that is a refundable deposit which is returned when the radio is brought back at the end of the day. The actual charge is thus only 100 yen.

I have one request. Please do not touch the shoulders or back of the rikishi, as they dislike this. I know you would like to touch them, but please refrain from doing so.

Once the day's bouts are over, please look up at the yagura outside. A yobidashi will be doing taiko there, and it would nice to listen to him for a bit.

In Conclusion

Through writing this book on sumo, I recalled many episodes from my career in the sumo world, which reinforced my perception that I have had both a sumo career and a yobidashi career.

When I stood on the dohyo as a yobidashi, I was always surrounded by spectators and sumo fans. Since I have retired, there have been people who have recognized me on the street and greeted me. This has made me very happy. Sumo is supported by fans like all of you. Please support rikishi, heya, and urakata (behind-the-scenes people in sumo) in the future.

I would like to take this opportunity to express my deepest gratitude to everyone in the sumo world for the great help they gave me over the years. I hope that the popularity of sumo will rise to even higher levels, and I sincerely hope for the continued development and success of the Nihon Sumo Kyokai.

Further, I would like to thank Ayako Suzuki-san, former manager in the public relations section of the Nihon Sumo Kyokai, Yasuhiro Kikuchi-san, President of Gendai Shokan, and sumo researcher Kenichi Koike-san, and Toshio Sakamoto-san, editor, for their assistance in making this book a reality.

December 2015

Hideo Yamaki

Bibliography

Sumo Daijiten (original work by Kanazashi Motoi, editorial supervision by Koeki Zaidan Hojin Nihon Sumo Kyokai, published by Gendai Shokan)

Ozumo Mankitsu Nyumon (Koeki Zaidan Hojin Nihon Sumo Kyokai)

Ozumo Pamphlet (Koeki Zaidan Hojin Nihon Sumo Kyokai)

Manga Ozumo Nyumonhen (Koeki Zaidan Hojin Nihon Sumo Kyokai)

Ozumo Gyoji no Sekai (by Hiromi Nema, published by Yoshikawa Kobunkan)

Rekishi Sansaku · Tokyo Edo Annai (by Masanobu Sakurai, published by Yasaka Shobo)

Glossary

B

banzuke (p. 64)
A ranking list of the rikishi*, gyoji*, and toshiyori* issued before each official tournament. Banzuke currently also list wakaimonogashira*, sewanin*, yobidashi* (jumaime* and above), and the tokoyama*. It is formally called the banzukehyo.

basho
This word is in daily use in the sumo world, and encompasses hombasho*, jungyo*, overseas exhibitions, etc. This also refers to the city or venue where a tournament is held. Further, the March tournament is refered to as the Osaka Basho, the July tournament as the Nagoya Basho and the November tournament as the Kyushu (Fukuoka) Basho (see hombasho).

beya (=heya) → sumo beya

C

chanko (p. 101)
Meals prepared by rikishi*, as well as meals consumed by rikishi, are called chanko. Chinese food, sashimi, and fried food are all known as chanko if eaten by rikishi.

chikaragami (p. 111)
Paper used by rikishi* to wipe their lips after rinsing their mouths with chikaramizu*, and also to brush off sweat. Although it is officially referred to as kami, it is also often called keshogami.

chikaramizu (p. 84)
Water rikishi* use to rinse their

mouths before the shikiri* and to purify their bodies. It is officially known as simply mizu.

D

dohyo (p. 32)
The place where rikishi* compete. This refers to both the trapezoid shape made from piled-up dirt, as well as the hanging roof above it.

dohyoiri (p. 104)
The ritual in which rikishi* line up on the dohyo* to be introduced to their audience (see yokozuna dohyoiri).

dohyo matsuri (p. 40)
A ritual of dedication and purification always held on the dohyo* on the day before the first day of official tournament.

E

eboshi (p. 69)
The black-lacquered cap worn by gyoji*.

F

fundoshi (p. 92)
A long, narrow cloth worn by men to cover the genital area (see mawashi).

G

gohei (p. 99)
Zigzag-shaped jute or paper streamers inserted into a rod. These streamers have long strips of white rectangle-shaped paper.

gunbai (p. 55, 69)
Gunbai are fan-shaped and are used by gyoji* to indicate the outcome of bouts.

gyoji (p. 14, 51, 55, 59, 62, 64, 67)
Gyoji officiate on the dohyo* for bouts between rikishi* of the east and west sides, and determine the winners. This word also refers to conducting such activities. All gyoji use the names of Kimura or Shikimori.

Glossary

H

hanamichi (p. 109)
The hanamichi is used by rikishi* to go back and forth from shitakubeya* to the dohyo*, and is also used by the shimpan (judge), gyoji*, and yobidashi* to enter and leave.

heya (=beya)
Heya is short for sumo beya*.

hiramaku (p. 88) → **maegashira**

hombasho
Official sumo tournaments, open to the public, regulated by the Nihon Sumo Kyokai (Japan Sumo Association), to measure the skill and ability of rikishi*. At present, there are six hombasho every year, held in Tokyo in January, May, and September, and chiho (regional) hombasho held in Osaka in March, Nagoya in July, and Fukuoka in November.

I

ichimon (p. 143)
A group of sumo beya* established by deshi (disciples) of a shisho* becoming independent and branching out to establish their own heya*.

J

jonidan (p. 82)
The division ranked below the sandanme* (see banzuke).

jonokuchi (p. 77, 82)
The division below the jonidan*, this being the lowest level listed on the banzuke* (see banzuke).

jumaime (=juryo) / (p. 19, 82)
The division below the makuuchi*. This is popularly referred to as the juryo*. Rikishi in the jumaime and above are called sekitori*. In other words, they are full-fledged rikishi (see sekitori).

jungyo (p. 127)
Sumo performances held in local

areas that are not hombasho* (see hombasho).

juryo (=jumaime) / (p. 19, 80)

K

kachikoshi (p. 87)
This refers to winning eight or more bouts in 15 day official tournaments in the jumaime* and above, or winning four or more bouts in the seven days rikishi* in the makushita* and below compete (see makekoshi).

kadoban (p. 89)
As ozeki* are demoted if they have makekoshi* records in two consecutive tournaments, they are referred to as being kadoban after the initial makekoshi record (see ozeki / makekoshi).

keiko (p. 48, 98, 162)
Sumo training which encompasses rikishi* excercising, learning the basic techniques, and mastering offensive and defensive tactics.

keikoba (p. 79, 99, 138)
The dohyo* which every heya* has for keiko* (see sumo beya).

keiko mawashi (p. 93)
The type of mawashi* used by rikishi* for keiko* (see mawashi).

kensho (p. 115, 127)
Prize money provided only for makuuchi* bouts by corporations or supporting groups for rikishi*, after applying to the Sumo Kyokai (see kenshokin).

kenshokin (p. 122)
Monetary awards given to the winners of bouts where there are kensho*.

keshomawashi (p. 85, 96, 104)
Apron-like ceremonial mawashi* for the dohyoiri*, which are used by rikishi* in the jumaime* and above. They have designs, patterns, or logos in the lower part, which reaches toward the ground (see mawashi).

Glossary

kimarite (p. 117)
The winning technique used by the victor in a bout.

koenkai (p. 141, 162)
Organizations which are formed to support either individual rikishi* or gyoji*, or sumo beya*.

komusubi (p. 88)
Rikishi* in the rank below sekiwake* (see makuuchi / sanyaku).

M

maegashira (p. 87, 123)
This refers to the makuuchi* rikishi* ranked below komusubi*, comprising of rikishi at maegashira 1 down to the lowest maegashira rank. To differentiate between komusubi and above, they are referred to as hiramaku* (see makuuchi).

maezumo (p. 65, 77)
Rikishi* who have passed the shindeshi* kensa (physical test for new recruits). This also refers to bouts in hombasho* between rikishi at this level (see shindeshi).

mage (p. 70)
The mage (topknots) in which the hair of rikishi* is arranged, using a motoyui (paper cord). This word also refers to all kinds of topknots (see tokoyama).

makekoshi (p. 88)
This refers to losing eight or more bouts in 15 day official tournaments in the jumaime* and above, or losing four or more bouts in the seven days rikishi* in the makushita* and below compete (see kachikoshi).

makushita (p. 83)
The rikishi in the division below the jumaime*. It is officially called the makushita nidanme (see tsukebito).

makuuchi (p. 122)
The highest division on the banzuke*, which includes the yo-

kozuna*, ozeki*, sekiwake*, komusubi*, and maegashira* (see kensho).

mawashi (p. 92)
This is a general term which includes shimekomi* and keiko mawashi*, etc. It is also sometimes referred to as mitsu* (see keshomawashi).

mitsu → **mawashi**
Another word for mawashi*.

mukojomen (p. 35)
This refers to the area of the dohyo* between the akabusa (red tassel) and shirobusa (white tassel), and is opposite to shomen* (see shomen).

N
nakairi
This refers to the intermission between the end of the jumaime* bouts and the beginning of the makuuchi* bouts. This intermission is used for the makuuchi dohyoiri, yokozuna dohyoiri*, and a changing of the judges.

O
oichomage (p. 70)
The type of topknot used by rikishi* in the jumaime* and above (see mage).

okamisan (p. 139)
The name by which rikishi* call the wife of the master of their heya* (see sumo beya / shisho).

oyakata (p. 134, 136)
The popular term for toshiyori* belonging to the Sumo Kyokai. The official term is toshiyori (see toshiyori).

ozeki (p. 88)
The rank below yokozuna* (see kadoban / makuuchi / sanyaku).

R
rikishi
This refers to men who engage in sumo professionally. They are

Glossary

only given this term after they have passed the Sumo Kyokai's physical test for new recruits, and been registered.

S
-san
An honorific attached to names of people.

sandanme (p. 83)
The division below the makushita* nidanme. There are individual ranks in the division, such as sandanme 2 or sandanme 3, and the higher the number means the lower the rank in the division (see makushita).

sanyaku
The ozeki*, sekiwake*, and komusubi* are generally referred to as the sanyaku.

seigen jikan (p. 113)
This is the time for the shikiri*, up to the moment when the two rikishi* synchronize their movements and clash at the tachiai*. It is formally referred to as a shikiri seigen jikan (the time limit for shikiri). Sometimes it's simply called jikan.

sekitori (p. 82)
This is an honorific title for rikishi* in the jumaime* and above. It can also be used collectively (see tsukebito / -zeki).

sekiwake (p. 88)
The rank below ozeki* (see makuuchi / sanyaku).

senshuraku
The final day of a sumo tournament. This is sometimes also called rakubi or raku.

sewanin (p. 14, 73)
Former makuuchi, jumaime*, or makushita* rikishi, who are hired by the Sumo Kyokai to manage the operation and transport of equipment for tournaments and other events (see wakaimono-

gashira).

shikiri (p. 36, 53, 112)
The two competing rikishi* face each other on the dohyo*, sufficiently touch the dohyo with both hands, and then synchronize their respiration in preparation for the tachiai*. This also refers to the related postures and stances (see seigen jikan).

shiko (p. 78, 98)
This is one of the key movements of sumo. Please refer to the illustration on p.79. On the dohyo*, the rikishi* do shiko by raising their left and then right legs in succession three times before starting the shikiri*. This word also refers to an important keiko* exercise to strengthen one's lower body (see suriashi / teppo).

shikona (p. 90)
The names of rikishi* (see shiko).

shimekomi (p. 93)
The formal term for the silk mawashi* worn by rikishi* in the jumaime* and above for bouts in hombasho*. It is popularly called mawashi (see mawashi).

shindeshi (p. 76)
Rikishi* who have just passed the physical examination for new recruits. This term also refers to rikishi with very little experience on the dohyo*. New rikishi are usually called shindeshi for about a year after they enter sumo, however, the formal term is rikishi yoseiin (trainee rikishi) / (see maezumo).

shisho (p. 136)
Toshiyori* who operate their own heya* are generally called shisho (masters). They are also known as oyakata* (see toshiyori).

shitakubeya (p. 74, 109)
The rooms where all rikishi* wait before the dohyoiri* and their

bouts. They also use the rooms to change before and after their bouts. The official term is rikishi hikaeshitsu (changing room for rikishi).

shitate (p. 113)
In a yotsu* position, this refers to the arm of a rikishi* who gets a grip below his opponent's side (see uwate / yotsu).

shobu shimpan (p. 58)
Judges for bouts in hombasho*. The formal term is shimpaniin. The judge who sits on the eastern part of the mukojomen* side is referred to as the tokeigakari, or timekeeper.

shomen (p. 35)
This refers to the area between the blue and black tassels hung above the northeast and northwest corners of the dohyo*. The head judge sits in front of the shomen side. The side opposite from shomen is called mukojomen*, with the east side on the left and the west side on the right. The east and west sides of the dohyo are designed without reference to actual geography (see mukojomen).

sumo beya (=heya) (p. 136, 162)
The units which are assigned by the Nihon Sumo Kyokai to raise rikishi*. This includes the personal residence and keikoba* of the shisho*, and is also where the rikishi live.

suriashi (p. 78, 98)
This is one of the fundamental movements of sumo and can be translated as sliding feet. Please refer to the illustration on p.79. In performing this exercise, one's feet move in a sliding movements, and do not leave the surface of the dohyo* (see shiko/ teppo).

T

tachiai (p. 114, 118)
The initial charge after the shiki-

ri*, when both rikishi* have synchronized their movements, this is just a brief movement before the bout starts. The tachiai or initial charge is vital as it is often said to determine the outcome of bouts.

tachimochi (p. 97, 105)
The rikishi* in the yokozuna dohyoiri* who carries the sword (see tsuyuharai).

taiko (p. 27)
Taiko (drumming) performed to make people aware of a sumo performance, is also done at critical junctures during the day. Drumming is an essential element of sumo (see yobidashi).

tattsukebakama (p. 16)
One of the types of men's formal divided skirts (please refer to the illustration on p.1) used by the yobidashi* and dekata during hombasho*. It takes on a tubular form from the knees downwards, and gives leeway around the hips.

teppo (p. 78, 98)
Thrusting against a pillar or wallboard in the keikoba* (with one's palms open). This is one of the exercises in keiko* and is intended to break an opponent's posture. Please refer to the illustration on p.79 (see shiko/ suriashi).

tokoyama (p. 14, 70)
Professionals employed by the Sumo Kyokai to arrange the hair of rikishi*. They are assigned to the heya* (see mage).

tokudawara (p. 35)
Four special bales protruding at about the width of one bale from each of the four sides; front, back, east and west.

torikumihyo (p. 26)
The list of all bouts from the jonokuchi* upwards. It is printed on A3 size paper and is given to all spectators. The records of the

Glossary

rikishi* in the top 15 ranks of the makushita* and above, as of the previous day, are printed on the back of the sheet.

toshiyori (p. 134)
Former rikishi* who assume a toshiyori myoseki (toshiyori name) after they retire. They are usually referred to as oyakata*. Their duty is to train deshi (disciples) / (see oyakata).

tsukebito (p. 85)
A rikishi* in the makushita* or other lower divisions who is assigned to a sekitori* in the jumaime* and above, and assists him personally. The word wakaimon is also used.

tsuyuharai (p. 97, 105)
The rikishi* in the yokozuna dohyoiri* who walks in front of the yokozuna* and symbolically clears the way (see tachimochi).

U
uwate (p. 113)
When rikishi* are in a yotsu* position, one rikishi gets his arms above those of his opponent. This word also refers to arms in an upper position (see shitate / yotsu).

W
wakaimonogashira (p. 14, 73)
Former makuuchi, jumaime* or makushita* rikishi, who are hired by the Sumo Kyokai to manage trainee rikishi* as well as other duties (see sewanin).

Y
yagura (p. 28)
A high wooden tower for doing taiko* built at the place where the sumo bouts are held (see taiko).

yobidashi
One of the types of behind-the-scenes people in sumo whose three main duties are to call out rikishi*, construct the dohyo*,

and do drumming (taiko*).

yokozuna
The highest rank in sumo (see makuuchi).

yokozuna dohyoiri (p. 105)
The dohyoiri* performed by yokozuna*, in which they are accompanied by tachimochi* and tsuyuharai*. This ceremony is performed after the makuuchi* dohyoiri in nakairi* on each day of hombasho*. The yokozuna dohyoiri is not simply a series of movements, but rather is one of the fundamental elements of sumo, and includes ancient shinto rites to pray for peace in the land and for good harvests (see tachimochi / tsuyuharai).

yotsu (p. 112)
When both rikishi in a bout come to grips on the mawashi*. Please refer to the illustration on p.112 (see shitate / uwate).

yumitorishiki (p. 119)
After the end of each day's bouts, a rikishi* designated to perform this rite receives a bow from the tategyoji, then performs the ceremony according to the site format. The yumitori rikishi is usually ranked in the makushita* or below.

Z
-zeki
An honorific added to the names of sekitori* (see sekitori).

Profile of Author

Former Tate Yobidashi Hideo Yamaki

Born in 1949 in Shimoda-shi, Shizuoka-ken.
His real name is Hidehito Yamaki.
He initially joined Isegahama Beya, was subsequently transferred to
Kiriyama Beya, and finally belonged to Asahiyama Beya.
Yobidashi Hideo made his debut in the March 1969 tournament.
After Yobidashi Yasuo reached retirement age after the July 2003 tournament,
Hideo became his successor as the top yobidashi
from the September 2003 tournament,
and thereafter called the final bout of each day during tournaments.
Yobidashi Hideo reached retirement age himself on December 27, 2014.

March 1969 tournament   Made his debut as an Isegahama Beya yobidashi.
July 1994 tournament   Was listed as a jumaime yobidashi
    when the yobidashi were listed on the banzuke.
January 1996 tournament   Promoted to makuuchi yobidashi.
May 2002 tournament   Promoted to sanyaku yobidashi.
January 2004 tournament   Promoted to fukutate yobidashi.
March 2007 Moved to Kiriyama Beya after Isegahama Beya closed.
January 2008 tournament   Promoted to tate yobidashi.
May 2011 Moved to Asahiyama Beya after Kiriyama Beya closed.
November 2014 tournament   Final tournament as a yobidashi.

Discover Sumo
Stories from Yobidashi Hideo

2017年1月8日　第1版第1刷発行
2025年1月10日　第1版第2刷発行

山木秀男 著

©2016, Hideo Yamaki
©2017, GENDAI SHOKAN PUBLISHING CO., LTD.

Publishing office:
GENDAI SHOKAN PUBLISHING CO., LTD.
3-2-5 Iidabashi Chiyoda-ku, Tokyo 102-0072 Japan
Tel: +81-(0)3-3221-1321   Fax: +81-(0)3-3262-5906

Printed by:
Hirakawa Kogyosha Co., Ltd.
Tokoinsatsujo

Binder:
Sekishindo Co., Ltd.

Translator:
Clyde Newton

Proofreader:
Teiko Sato

Illustrator:
Ayamorikemuri

Book design:
Shigeaki Ito

Printed in Japan   ISBN978-4-7684-5798-6
定価はカバーに表示してあります。
乱丁・落丁本はおとりかえいたします。
禁無断転載
The price is indicated on the cover.
Any copies with damage or missing pages will be replaced.
All rights reserved